WORCESTERSHIRE'S
WAR

Voices of the First World War

WORCESTERSHIRE'S
WAR

Adrian Gregson, John Peters & Maggie Andrews

AMBERLEY

First published 2014

Amberley Publishing
The Hill, Stroud
Gloucestershire, GL5 4EP

www.amberley-books.com

British Library Cataloguing in Publication Data.
A catalogue record for this book is available from the British Library.

ISBN 978 1 4456 3445 6 (hardback)
ISBN 978 1 4456 3452 4 (ebook)

Typesetting and Origination by Amberley Publishing
Printed in Great Britain

Contents

Introduction

This book is only a starting point for those interested in the history of Worcestershire during the First World War. The commemorative activities which mark the 100th anniversary of the First World War will continue until November 2018, providing an opportunity to learn, engage, educate, entertain and remember. Projects are being run all over the UK, not just in Worcestershire. Many of them encourage people to come forward with their diaries, letters, photographs and stories of their grandparents and great-grandparents and their experience of the war – at home or on a fighting front. By doing this we will enrich the amount of information around and provide real insight for research into not just the units, the formations, the tactics and the generals, but the people who were actually there, who were involved directly. For information – specifically the organisations, events and opportunities linked to the Worcestershire World War One Hundred Project – see: www.ww1worcestershire.co.uk.

Voices of War and Peace: The Great War and its Legacy is a new First World War Engagement Centre funded by the Arts & Humanities Research Council in partnership with the Heritage Lottery Fund. The University of Birmingham centre is a joint initiative with Birmingham City University, Newman University, the University of Wolverhampton and the University of Worcester. The Engagement Centre is based in the Library of Birmingham and will support a wide range of community engagement activities, connecting academic and public histories of the First World War as part of the commemoration of the war's centenary, which begins in 2014. The centre covers a broad range of relevant research knowledge that will enable it to respond to diverse community interests. This research knowledge ranges from the history of Birmingham, the Black Country and urban and rural Worcestershire to the impact of air power, from the experiences of Belgian refugees to trench warfare, from Quakers and humanitarian relief to battlefield archaeology, and from caring for the casualties of war to the involvement of colonial troops and labour. Voices of War and Peace: The Great War and its Legacy offers research support and guidance for community groups around the First World War in general and in particular around the following themes: Belief and the Great War, Childhood, Cities at War, Commemoration and Gender and the Home Front. www.voicesofwarandpeace.org.

The Imperial War Museum is also acting as a coordinator of national and local events. For further information please visit: www.iwm.org.uk/centenary.

1

Worcestershire and the Outbreak of War

Most historians of Worcestershire in the nineteenth and early twentieth centuries agree that the county was varied in nature and environment. Behind a veneer of black-and-white villages and attractive riverside towns containing much of the history of the English Civil Wars was a fertile county, but one bounded by the Malvern Hills – one of the oldest mountain ranges in the world – the Cotswolds, and the industry of Greater Birmingham. Its agricultural fertility was based around the rivers Severn and Avon with orchards, hops, wheat and barley being particularly prevalent. Farming covered the range, from cattle and dairy, pigs, sheep and poultry to arable and especially market gardening. Country life was enriched through cricket, the races in Worcester, point-to-point and foxhunting.[1] Industry was concentrated in the city and to the north, and was surprisingly extensive. China, gloves and of course sauce in Worcester; carpets in Kidderminster; salt at Droitwich; glass and bricks in Stourbridge; needles and fish hooks in Redditch; nails at Bromsgrove; and coal and iron around Bewdley.[2]

Worcestershire's character was fashioned in part by the pre-Reformation Church as a great landowner,[3] but the county aristocracy owned significant acres, houses and lands and controlled tenants across the great estates, including Beauchamp at Madresfield, Lyttelton and Hagley, Coventry at Croome, Pakington in Westwood Park, Southwell at Hindlip, Sandys of Ombersely, Foley in Kidderminster and Lechmere at the Rhydd.[4] Things were not necessarily so good, however, on the outbreak of war. Acreage of hops and market gardening increased while wheat was on the decline.[5] Wages increased slightly but food costs rose by 25 per cent, nullifying that effect.[6] Ironically, the improved life and living conditions and the rise in educational standards was pulling people away from the agricultural life and causing a depression for those agricultural labourers left behind. On the other hand, technical innovations were driving a new agricultural revolution. Bomfords were making engines for reapers and threshers while Thomas' of Worcester were producing wind-pumping engines, exporting out of the county.[7]

If their lives before 1914 had been characterised by the following description in the 1889 *County Guide*, they were certainly in for a rude awakening when the war came. 'From the accession of George III, Worcestershire has been in the happy position of having had no history, and in the still happier one of having none among its inhabitants who have made any … she has settled down into an ordinary county.'[8] The involvement of the inhabitants of Worcestershire in the war, at home and in battle, was to change all that.

The growing international crisis started to take effect as the August Bank Holiday weekend began. The Great Western Railway placed a notice in the newspaper to say that all their excursions and cheap bookings for the following Tuesday would be cancelled and the Post Office announced reported changes to its routines. By the second week of August local newspapers were preoccupied by the war, and also reported that the Perdiswell Show had been cancelled, the Worcester Music Festival postponed and pigeon racing disrupted.[9] Letters to the editor suggest that men over thirty should form a local contingent of the Home Guard, and there were pleas for good-quality horses for the Army. It was also reported that, at the newly opened Silver cinema, 'Anything dealing with the war aroused the audience to great cheering. "Europe in Arms" had an ovation and a picture of the Kaiser came in for cat calls.'[10]

The cricket season was suspended but football continued for the full season, though not beyond. Worcester City commenced the 1914/15 season as the reigning Birmingham and District League champions and in a sound financial position. They were able to retain most of the side from the previous season, although a couple of their best players had moved onto bigger clubs. Meanwhile a decision was taken to cancel the local amateur football leagues as many of the clubs were unable to field a team due to so many local men signing up to join the forces – conversely, one of the reasons for keeping football going was the opportunity to recruit from among the crowds. Recruitment activities went on throughout the county and this notice in the *Worcester Daily Times* was typical of the publicity:

TO THE
MEN OF ENGLAND
with Staunch Brave Hearts
PREVENT
CONSCRIPTION
BY
VOLUNTEERING NOW.
To Protect the World from
Military Aggression and Oppression,
and Save Yourselves also.[11]

In Kidderminster it was the start of the annual shut-down, and most local mills were reported to be on holiday for the Bank Holiday week.[12] The next week, the Kidderminster Shuttle reported a run on provisions and a list of carpet factories and spinning mills who had stood idle: Brinton's, Humphries, Woodward and Grosvenor, and Naylor. Only the Caldwell Spinning Mill ran, though it was difficult getting bales from Liverpool and London due to the railways being held up. The following week the 'Carpet Trade' report stated that due to the threat to wages and livelihoods, the big companies had agreed to run a three-day week. Meanwhile, the head of the Brinton family

Recently enlisted men. (With thanks to Worcestershire Archive and Archaeology Service)

and his wife had gone missing somewhere in Europe, on their way to Stockholm, via Berlin and Moscow.[13]

One historian identified the Malverns as being the key thing that bound a Worcestershire identity, it being the 'most significant, most noticeable from all aspects of the county'.[14] Was this what the soldiers, entrenched in Flanders or Gallipoli, or in the sands of Egypt, thought of when they thought of 'Home'? Malvern itself was quick to get on a war footing and on Saturday 8 August 1914 the Malvern Urban District Council met to discuss how to organise local resources to meet the emergency of war. The range of committees they set up indicates an awareness of the potential disruption to everyday life that war would bring, and included: the General Committee for Public Safety, a sub-committee on food supply, another to ascertain the occupants of every house and their minimum needs, one on emergency relief and yet another on emergency measures. The committees were made up of those on the council and 'zealous' citizens, and liaised with the local Red Cross.[15]

As a large, rural county, Worcestershire had not only a county regiment but also the Yeomanry cavalry. In addition to the four Regular battalions of the regiment were the two main Territorial battalions – 7th and 8th Worcestershires – with recruiting bases in Worcester, Evesham and Kidderminster. On 3 August the Chairman of the Worcestershire Territorial Association wrote to *Worcester Daily Times*:

TO THE EDITOR

Sir – there is a deficiency in the Territorial Forces of this Country of 259 men, of which Worcester contributes: – Yeomanry 31, RFA 19 and Infantry 57. Redditch RFA 47, Infantry 31. Kidderminster: RFA 10, Infantry 30 and there are smaller deficiencies in other places.

I am therefore writing to you to make these facts public in the hope of inducing Recruiting Committees in all places, especially those mentioned, to become particularly active in the matter of obtaining recruits for the Territorial Force of this County in view of the very grave situation of Europe. May I hope, also that those who are in a position to actively join in the defence of their country may not let so important an occasion pass of proving the patriotism of the Loyal County of Worcester is no idle boast.

RC Temple
Chairman of the Worcestershire Territorial Association[16]

On the outbreak of war many indeed flocked to the colours of their local unit of these Territorial battalions. The 5th and 6th battalions of the 'Special Reserve' were primarily for training and providing recruits to the four Regular battalions. The 1st Battalion Worcestershire Regiment was in Egypt in August 1914, returning to England in October, and so it was that the first foray into the war was carried by the men of the 2nd and 3rd Battalions.[17] The British Expeditionary Force started moving over to France a few days after war was declared, beginning on 9 August. Orders for Worcestershire were received the following week and by 14 August the 2nd Battalion was in Boulogne, joining the 2nd Division. At the same time, the 3rd Battalion landed at Le Havre and sailed up the Seine to Rouen. From there, both battalions were entrained and then marched to the front, where on 23 August the BEF was concentrated around the town of Mons. The combined forces of the French and British were unable to withstand the German offensive and so began the retirement known as 'The Retreat from Mons', beginning at Frameries, Ciply, Mormal and Le Cateau until the British were able to turn the Germans into retreat at the Battle of the Marne.

Private Wheatley, of Hallow, was injured by a shell during the retreat:

It is the aeroplanes which do the damage. They drop white powder which explodes and shows where we are, and then the shells come along, six or seven at a time. You can hear them coming in the air, and your anxiety is in the waiting to see where they will burst. All the injuries were caused by their shrapnel. Their infantry fire is practically useless. They run along with their rifles on their hips but they cannot aim. The only bullet I heard of which hit the mark was one which struck one of our men in the forehead. It went straight through his head. He was a Birmingham man and the first one in 3rd Worcesters who was killed.[18]

Both battalions were part of an almost continual period of movement, with the advance continuing for the 2nd Battalion on 13 September at the Battle of the Aisne. The first rest they took in billets was on 21 September, while it was several more days before the 3rd Battalion could rest. The fighting on the Aisne was particularly vicious, with much of it hand-to-hand over trenches. A sergeant in the 2nd Battalion Worcestershire Regiment wrote from hospital for the paper:

Soon we saw coming out of the inky darkness a long line of white faces and in response to the quick order we fired right into them. The first line wavered for a moment or two, part of it was blotted out but the line of reserves behind filled up the gaps and the front line advanced again, seeming not to heed the heavy hail of bullets we were pouring into them.

Just about one hundred yards off our trenches the first line of advancing Germans flung themselves flat on the earth, fixing bayonets while the second fired over their heads and yet a third line was pushing forward men to fill the gaps of the second line where our fire tore through. Then the first line rose, and the second fixed bayonets also. Finally they all came sweeping forward with the bayonet and threw themselves right into our trenches. We poured one terrible volley into them as they came on but all the devils in hell couldn't have stopped them.

Our front ranks gave way slightly before the fierceness of the attack and the weight of men hurled at them, but the recoil was only temporary. We steadied ourselves and while they were standing still for a moment to take breath and dress their ranks for another rush we went at them with the bayonet, and hurled them over the trenches down the hill again. It was in this rush that I got run through with a bayonet.[19]

By the end of September there was an uneasy lull with neither side ready to commit to attack, during which time the British Expeditionary Force was moved further north, more clearly to defend the Channel ports, and both Worcestershire battalions were marched to the flatlands of Flanders.[20] From the middle of October, the 3rd Battalion was engaged in the Lys Valley area and the Battle of La Bassée when they were moved into the 5th Division. The month was largely spent fighting and establishing a narrow trench line from Aubers to Givenchy and Neuve Chapelle; during this period there were over 300 casualties.

According to Stacke, the two Reserve battalions, 5th and 6th, mobilised and moved to war stations around Plymouth. They did vital work on the coast but also acted as holding organisations for convalescing soldiers waiting to return to their units. Their composition was therefore constantly in flux.[21]

The two Territorial battalions, 1/7th and 1/8th, saw a rapid recruitment drive in August, so much so that very soon, second lines of both battalions were being signed up. Initially, recruitment for the Territorial Force was not to include overseas action, but this soon changed and volunteers were given a choice to return home or stay with the Colours. A third line was recruited in early 1915 to assist with home defence. Stacke is unusually critical of Lord Kitchener's call to arms in raising the 'New Armies' rather than relying on the existing county regiments. However, the Worcestershire Regiment had one New Army battalion for each of the three new divisions, in the 9th, 10th and 11th Worcestershire battalions. They were to be trained through 1914–1915, moving to the Western and Eastern Fronts in the summer months. Both Territorial battalions moved first to Swindon, then to Brentford and finally were based at Danbury, Essex. After spending the winter training, they were considered fit for the front in early 1915 and embarked to France on 31 March when they joined the many other ranks of Territorials in boosting the Regular BEF in France and Flanders.

A member of the *Malvern News* staff training in the 8th Battalion in Essex wrote to the Worcester paper with reports of their life. Private G. F. Gilbert's enthusiasm for training provokes some interesting comparisons with the accounts printed above of the actual fighting on the Aisne.

As the days go on our training becomes more and more interesting … we have battalion drill, trench digging, tactical exercises, night operations and the more practical side of infantry training.

Yesterday C Company made an attack on a neighbouring hill where the 'enemy' were supposed to be entrenched. When we came under artillery fire we deployed and advanced in that fashion until about 1,400 yards from the hill. We then extended, and when we were within about 200 yards and enemy bullets were whistling overhead, we made a terrific charge with fixed bayonets, cheering all the way.[22]

The Worcestershire Yeomanry – volunteer soldiers like those in the Territorial Force – had a similar experience before they made it to the battlefronts. In their case the destination was to be the Near and Middle East, before ending up in the trenches of the Western Front. The Worcestershire Yeomanry recruited its squadrons from its Worcester HQ, but also from Malvern, Birmingham and Kidderminster. Commanders of the three war footing squadrons were Major Hugh Cheape, Major Charles Coventry and Captain John (Jack) Lyttelton, the Liberal-Unionist MP for Droitwich. In the 1st South Midlands Mounted Brigade – later called the 5th Mounted Brigade – they joined Yeomanry forces with Warwickshire and Gloucestershire under General E. A. Wiggin.[23]

Before the war they had followed the pattern of most county Yeomanry regiments, certainly since the Haldane Army Reforms of 1908. All volunteers, albeit with some veterans of previous campaigns in South Africa, their training was largely restricted to an annual camp. In 1907 they were at Croome Court; in 1908, Blackmore Park near Malvern. However, from the following year until 1913 they had encamped on Salisbury Plain.[24] With a new and younger commander in Lord Dudley, a plan of rejuvenation and more intense training was in hand. This had begun with a small cadre of NCOs and other ranks, but before a full Yeomanry training camp could be held in 1914, war was declared and the unit mobilised. That meant that their last training together had been nearly fifteen months previously. This explains in part why they remained in England for so long after mobilisation. Joining other Yeomanry divisions at Warwick, they trained at Bury St Edmunds and Norwich and subsequently near Newbury, and then for four months in King's Lynn, before embarking from Avonmouth on 10 December 1914.

Victor Godrich, a mounted cavalryman who had joined the Territorial Army as a volunteer in 1905, recalled his memory of the first days of war.

On 3rd August 1914: I was to be found on Sutton Park Rifle Range near Kidderminster, where the Regimental Musketry competitions were in progress. It was a very enjoyable little camp. The weather was fine, the company good and altogether was a far better way of spending the weekend than mixing with the crowds at some seaside town. The shooting for the Regimental Cup was fixed for Bank Holiday Monday, 4th August. I was proud to be shooting in my Squadron's team for the first time. We were almost through with the shoot when a messenger came up with a telegram which he handed to the Adjutant, Captain Leslie Cheape. There was a great deal of tension in the air, I recollect. We were all expecting something.

Captain Cheape opened the telegram and read out to us that War had been declared. We were to break up camp at once and hurry back to our homes. What a waste of time everyone thought at once. Here we are in uniform with our rifles and ammunition, why not get across to France straight away, what else did we want? We had a lot to learn in those days. What excitement we all felt. What discussions we had with our threats to the German Army for daring to fight England.

How we crowded round old Sergeant Major Downes and plied him with questions. Did he think we would get a look-in at this little campaign that had just commenced, or would it all be over before we had our horses and equipment? Jack was a wise old bird for he assured us that it would last much longer than we thought, undoubtedly we should be wanted.

We packed up and left Kidderminster that day. On the Tuesday I went to the office and put in a full day. I am afraid that most of it was spent discussing the situation, already I was feeling proud to have a uniform to get into, which was much better than being a 'mere civilian'. Tuesday night there was only one place to go. That of course was Squadron Headquarters where I found a very noisy, busy crowd. Two or three were assisting Sergeant Major Osborne to send out 'mobilisation notices', the remainder were demanding buttons, pull-throughs and other important things at this critical time.

We received our notices on Wednesday morning 6th August 1914 warning us that we were called upon 'to present ourselves at Squadron Headquarters at 9.00 am and were under direct penalties should we fail to put in an appearance'. At 10.00 am we gathered to meet for the first time Major Hugh Gray-Cheape who had been posted to Command B Squadron. We drew everything that Sergeant Major Osborne had to issue. At 2.00 pm we entrained at Camp Hill Station for Worcester, speeded by a large crowd of loving Mothers, Sisters and sweethearts. I need hardly say that there were wet eyes in the crowd. The most brutal thing of all now took place. We were lined up on the platform and our Identification Discs were handed out. We had to tell the girls that they were given to us to wear in case we were blown to pieces, thus our corpses could be identified.

Well, wasn't it likely to be the finishing touch to a sad farewell![25]

Not all of the Yeomanry could leave their jobs as quickly as Victor Godrich. The *Worcester Daily Times* enthusiastically reported on 4 September:

EXCEPTIONAL RECRUITS FOR YEOMANRY

Up to this morning 100 men have been accepted to fill the vacancies in the Worcestershire Yeomanry, caused by men who cannot go on foreign service. It is expected that the 200 necessary will be enrolled before the end of next week, the first hundred having come in less than a week. These hundred men, all of whom have passed the very severe riding test, are a splendid body of young fellows. A good proportion are farmer's sons, and most bear the traces of a healthy, open air life. Already they are for the most part physically fit so that their military training can start immediately. Major Eric Knight, M.P., the Officer Commanding the Depot, has expressed his great pleasure at the exceptional lot of recruits who have passed through his hands, He says he had never seen a finer body of young fellows. The first 100 will join the Regiment now quartered in on of Southern counties on Monday.[26]

The heightened tension caused by the declaration of war was felt at all levels of society in Worcestershire. A concern, propagated through the press, that Britain was awash with spies even made its way to the villages of the Cotswolds. Mary Anderson, a retired actress living in Broadway, remembered the first days of the war when her husband and children left home to contribute to the war effort in various ways while writing her autobiography in the 1930s:

Our boy – not yet twenty-one – had joined the United Arts Rifles, but was eventually invalided out. Tony was still not well. Our men servants had left for war service. I was alone with a staff of women, expecting daily to see the Germans march down Broadway Hill and demolish us, and always on the outlook for German spies!

One day, talking to a friend in the road, I saw a man, looking to my mind like a typical German spy, pass our house, come back and stand gazing at it. I told my friend I was sure the suspicious-looking individual was a spy. 'I will speak to him, and if his accent is German, ring up the police.' My friend begged me not to do so, saying: 'He is a spy, I am sure, and he will shoot you as soon as you approach him.' With my heart in my feet I walked up to him and said, smiling: 'My watch has stopped, will you please tell me the time?' With an undoubted Western American accent he pulled out his watch: 'I guess my watch has gone a bit crazy in this damp country; it says half-twelve.' I thanked him, feeling very foolish. He smiled and said: 'Say! this is our Mary's house, ain't it?' 'No, it is Mr. de Navarro's house.' 'Well I never! I have walked all the way up here to see her house and, Miss Mary, I guess this is your house all right, so be a good fellow and own up.' That little episode cured me of the spy-fever, but my fears of an invasion led me into putting Tony's hats into various front windows and to accept from a friend a huge bull-mastiff which looked like a lioness and was called 'Tiger'. The sight of 'Tiger' terrified everyone, visitors and tradespeople fled from him, but with me he was a gentle, slobbering animal. When on a lead he nearly tore my arms from their sockets, but he fulfilled his job, and held everyone at bay – a huge, magnificent brute.[27]

At the end of October, the 2nd Battalion was to be involved in a battle that became the defining moment for the regiment as a whole, and the home community. Gheluvelt is a small suburb of Ypres and, in October 1914, the Germans attempted to break through the British line near Gheluvelt Chateau. On 31 October they were successful, taking Gheluvelt and opening up a gap in the British defences. What became known as the First Battle of Ypres opened up in October 1914 with the 2nd Battalion Worcestershire Regiment in the 2nd Division advance, which began on 21 October to take Langemarck. The advance halted, and German bombardment caused extensive casualties among the now entrenched troops. They withdrew from the position on 24 October with a new plan to counter-attack at Polygon Wood, an attack which was eventually mounted the following day along with a series of new attacks over the next few days, until the 2nd Worcestershires were back in reserve on 30 October.

The next day, an intense attack by the enemy broke the British line by midday. Despite being at the front for ten days of intense fighting, the men of the 2nd Battalion were virtually the last men standing, and so, while the British guns were moved back in readiness for a general retreat, the Worcestershire men were propelled into a counter-attack. The details of how the enemy was routed that afternoon are well documented by Stacke. The battalion was joined in its stand by the South Wales Borderers, more by luck than judgement, but nonetheless it proved vital assistance. One-third of the Worcestershire Battalion was lost on 31 October and after a day's fighting, despite the gap being held, British forces were withdrawn to a new trench line that was to remain almost the same for the next four years. The significance of the action was not immediately apparent to the people at home. At an inspection of the battalion in November, the commander-in-chief, Field Marshall Sir John French, said,

On 31st October, we were in a very critical position. At headquarters we received the report that the village of Gheluvelt, an extremely important strategic point, had been taken by the enemy. Matters looked very critical. Shortly after, I was informed that the village of

21

Gheluvelt had been re-captured by a counter attack. Since then I have made repeated inquiries as to what Officer was responsible for the conduct of this counterstroke, and have invariably received the reply that it was the Worcestershire Regiment who carried out this attack. I have, therefore, in my dispatch to the Secretary of State, so mentioned it, and said it was the Worcestershire Regiment who took the action in relieving this critical state. You bear on your colours the names of many famous victories, and in this war you have added lustre to your former reputation.[28]

His statement was reported to Worcestershire County Council in December, and the council agreed that copies thereof should be sent to all the schools in the county, with a request that it be read by the head teacher at the next meeting of the school, and that copies should also be sent to the chairmen of the parish councils in the county, with a request that they should take steps to make it known throughout the parishes.[29] The following year, schools were also issued with a booklet by the county council entitled *How the Worcesters Saved the Day*, which provided a graphic description of the battle.[30] The reputation of the Worcestershires and the almost mythical significance of the Battle of Gheluvelt grew even during wartime; it was recounted in national and local newspapers across the country and described by some as one of the mysteries of the war. Speculation and rumour surrounded the question of who had given the order to attack. The *Birmingham Mail* carried a story the following year claiming it had received a letter from someone who described the following encounter on a train.

In the next seat was a passenger who knew who it was who gave the order to charge. He, a soldier private of Kidderminster, had been in France from August last, and had been in the charge, belonging as he did to the Worcesters. He was wounded by a shell at Neuve Chapelle and was returning from a Southampton Hospital.

He stated that Major Hankey gave the order and then after the depleted regiment formed, told the men not to say who gave it – whether out of modesty or reticence or for reasons that did not appear. But the glorious deed was certainly attributed to him according to the man who was one of the survivors.[31]

In 1917, on the anniversary of the battle, the event was again referred to in all schools in Worcestershire and students were asked to write an essay on the battle. The Chairman of the Education Committee offered prizes for the best essays,[32] and Colonel Hankey was given the freedom of the city of Worcester. Barbourne Park in Worcester was renamed in honour of the battle and in addition the council built a row of houses for soldiers' families immediately after the war. Sir John French officially 'opened' Gheluvelt Park in 1922 and the battle has remained a significant honour for the regiment for a hundred years.

2

The Yeomanry in the Middle East

Fighting a war in the Middle East, or indeed fighting a war against the Turks at all, had not been one of Britain's war aims in 1914. However, Turkey's involvement in the war on the side of Germany made the conflict inevitable. The Ottoman Empire, like the empires of the West, was on the wane in 1914; however, it did stretch south of Turkey to encompass the whole of Arabia, Syria, Mesopotamia, Egypt and Palestine. With their key interests in the Suez Canal, both France and Britain were keen to protect free passage to and from the Mediterranean and the rest of the British Empire. Although part of the Turkish Ottoman Empire, Egypt was in de facto control of the British and had been since the end of the previous century.[1] Since 1911, Turkey had been losing parts of its Balkan states to other countries, and the Triple Entente between France, Britain and Turkey's traditional enemy, Russia, had left her surrounded. Germany, on the other hand, had spent the years leading up to 1914 building up the Turkish fighting machine, since it faced enmity on so many fronts.[2] It was not until 2 November 1914 that Turkey was at war with Russia, and then from 5 November with Britain and France.[3] As a result of this, Britain had to mobilise forces in order to adequately defend and keep secure its interests in the region, including the canal and a number of oilfields.

The campaign variously described as Egypt, Palestine and Mesopotamia, depending on the particular area of intense activity at the time, was very different to those fought in France and Flanders. The key differences, of course, were the climate and terrain. Instead of a series of defensive trenches and the occasional attack, the campaigns in the deserts were fluid, front lines always changing, with much fewer casualties and still the use of real cavalry.[4] The background to a lot of the Allied troops was different too – Egypt became a staging and training post for troops from New Zealand and Australia, and also for the Indian Army. Some of these passed through to the Western Front, others remained in the Middle East. British troops scheduled to go to Egypt were originally planned to be Territorials, not Regulars.[5] Although this policy changed as the demands of the fighting were recognised, the mainstay of the Mediterranean Expeditionary Force remained Territorial and Yeomanry Units.

The Yeomanry cavalry of Worcestershire arrived at Alexandria on Egypt's Mediterranean coast in late April 1915, as part of the 2nd Mounted Division. During this first period in Egypt they trained and visited the sights, as well as assisting in the evacuation of the hospital ships pouring out of Gallipoli after the ill-fated landings of 25 April 1915.[6] By August they themselves were on the way to Suvla Bay. After a failed attack on Scimitar Hill they spent three months with little respite at Suvla, where dysentery and general illnesses cut into the troops.[7] After a month on Lemnos, they returned to Alexandria at the end of November with half the number of men that had left from there that August.[8]

Victor Godrich left behind his regular job in the General Post Office, and set sail for the Middle East as part of the Worcestershire Yeomanry on 11 April 1915. His recollections of his first experiences of war in the Middle East were written in the 1920s and 1930s.[9]

The soldiers boarded the 'SS Saturnia' and set sail around 4:00 pm on the 11 April. We soon discovered that we not considered 'First Class 'passengers and we learnt the art of sleeping in a hammock. The ship was overcrowded, the food atrocious. I often wondered how many millions Messrs. Donaldson 7 Co. (and other shipping companies) made by starving and overcrowding the men who had volunteered to defend England …

After our entry into the Mediterranean, most of us spent the nights on deck as the weather was very mild. On April 19th we coasted Tunisia and on 20th April we arrived at Malta.

On entering the Grand Harbour we passed several French battleships, which turned out their bands to play us in (Jules Ferry, Danton, Courbet and an old British Ship the Caesar). We responded with the Marseillaise, Tipperary etc in about a dozen different keys (unaccompanied).

In the afternoon we had permission to go ashore and had the most enjoyable time. We heard that Lord Windsor, who was on the Governor's staff obtained the privilege for us. Everybody's first thought was to have a good square meal as were half staved. We had a meal in one restaurant, promptly followed by a meal in another one. Malta was a lovely place. The harbour is surrounded with hills on which is built the town of Valetta.

They departed Malta the following day and arrived in the city of Alexandria on 24 April.

French influence was seen everywhere in the street names, in the advertisements, tradesman's signs, all in French – one looked in vain for a bit of English. We arrived at last at our camp, Chatby, and found that the horses had arrived the day before. We lost 26 animals on the voyage, which I suppose was not excessive. Chatby was a lovely position right on the edge of the sea with trains running close by.

We discovered that grass did not grow in Egypt: consequently our camp was soon very dusty … When the wind blew, one could not see 100 yards. We decided to explore the wonderful wicked city … [but] … It seemed too strange to be true. As the time went on the weather became hotter, we could do little during the day except bathe. Exercising horses of course had to done every day. This took place before breakfast and the route we followed was along the Mahmoudin Canal, which connects Alexandria with the Nile then round the Mouzha gardens – a beautifully kept public path where they actually grew good grazing grass.

Postcard from Alexandria.

Postcard from Alexandria.

For nearly three months the troops remained in Alexandria, enabling Victor to make a weekend visit to Cairo, which was only three and a half hours away by train. There was also the climate to get used to – he noted on one occasion in June that 'Kharmseen Wind was blowing like a furnace. Everything you touch burns your hands; clothes (shorts and shirt) weigh a ton'. He also had his first encounter with the Turkish soldiers on 8 May 1915:

We saw our first Turks, a boatload of prisoners who had arrived from the Dardenelles. We met and escorted them to the railway station – from there they were sent to Cairo. They struck me as a well-made lot of fellows who would give a good account of themselves.

His first experience of a death among his compatriots occurred at the end of July, when someone with heart trouble died while swimming; another was invalided home with jaundice. The reality of war slowly impinged, and he noted in early August that 'we now began to see another side of the story as parties of our men were sent down to the Docks to help unload wounded men who were constantly arriving'. On 1 August he observed,

We guessed that our first experience of war would be as Infantry and our destination we anticipated would be Gallipoli, Alexandria was the base for the Dardenelles operations. We constantly saw drafts of reinforcements leaving for the ill-fated peninsula.

The news was finally confirmed that they were to go to Gallipoli, and on 17 August:

We arrived at the island of Mudros and entered the harbour of Lemnos ... the harbour was full of ships of all sizes.

The Royal Edward was torpedoed a few miles from Lemnos the day before we arrived. The Royal Edward was loaded principally with hospital requisites – x-ray apparatus, medicines, etc.

It carried a large number of Nurses and RAMC personnel, many of whom were drowned. It was a severe blow to our Dardenelles Operation and the effects felt for many months afterwards when the bad weather arrived.

Lemnos became a huge graveyard many of the lads who had been injured on the peninsula died here from lack of attention or food.

I am sorry to say that many of the brave nursing women died also. After remaining on the 'Ascania' all day, we transferred to the Queen Victoria, a small paddle steamer that used to run tourists down the Thames to Margate.

They disembarked at night:

As we got ashore up the beach, the first thing I remember was the peculiar smell, which I shall remember all my life when I think of Gallipoli. It is the scrub that grows out east, mixed with the smell of death. I can recall that same smell again at Gaza, Beersheba, Kuwelfeh, Es Salt and several places where men had been killed. There is nothing like that sense of smell to refresh one's memory – that peculiar Gallipoli smell I shall always carry in my memory.

The next morning he came under fire for the first time:

I must confess that at the first taste of shellfire, I felt funky and wanted to find a hole anywhere out of the road but there was nowhere to go! The Turks began shelling the rest of the regiment who were coming ashore in barges. By watching men who had been ashore a few days one gained confidence.

The next few days involved marching with guns and ammunition and hearing the bombardment from battleships and guns. Then on 21 August 1915,

We advanced in Columns of Troops across an open plain with a hill about two miles ahead. Our objective was a good-sized hill which was named Chocolate Hill due to its dark brown colour. All went well till the leading brigade got half way across the plain, then all hell was let loose.

Shrapnel fell like hail, rifle fire like rain made gaps in our ranks. It was not a pleasant feeling to see a man dropping ahead of you knowing that you soon would be amongst it. The two miles or so we marched seemed the longest that I have ever travelled.

We came across several poor chaps who had finished their soldiering; they looked as though they were asleep, I met Billy Cruse returning with his thumb knocked off …

I remember thinking, amid all the noise, what a lot of things need picking up – helmets, rifles equipment. Some of the sights we saw were horrible, most of the damage from shrapnel or high explosive shells … I shall never forget a small fellow of the South Notts Yeomanry. He had been hit across the knuckles by a piece of shell, completely smashing his fingers. He was about 17 or 18 and very upset because he had lost his rifle.

After the battle they counted the dead and wounded and progressed on until on 23 of August.

Our first glimpse of trench life was not at all encouraging. Imagine a narrow ditch with sandbags on the side facing the enemy with a dirty, unshaven, hungry looking man every 300 yards; little holes in the side of the ditch with a dirty tin over a small fire where some poor devil was trying to make a drink of tea. The only occupation sleeping, making tea and standing up as your turn comes to look over the top and watch the enemy. War is a glorious pastime in books when you have the whole scheme laid out, the strategy explained and a map with a red line showing 'our position' marked. But to the poor beggars 'doing it' there is nothing but misery …

The days drag slowly on … War makes one very callous and inhuman. In the particular position we were at the time the outlook was ghastly although we had cleared the ground in front of the trench for 100 yards or so.

By early September, the fatalities, injuries, exhaustion and disease are beginning to take their toll. He notes,

On the Thursday night (2nd) we were ordered to post double sentries which meant Doug Lamb and Bylie being on sentry all night long.

I thought this was a bit thick, so about midnight I told them to get down and I did a turn myself, but I had overestimated my power and fell asleep and was awakened by an Irish officer doing the 'rounds'. (I discovered after he had reported me). Here with my rifle I walked to the edge of the trench and carefully chose my target and 'sniped' my first Turkish soldier, 700 yards distance from where I aimed.

He was court-martialled in a dugout by officers of his regiment. In reflecting upon it he asserted, 'Let a man who had been through the "hell of the trenches" judge me and I know what his verdict will be.' With Colonel Coventry's reference of his good character he felt he had the court's sympathy, and his punishment was to be reduced in rank to a private. However,

Trench life began to get on our nerves … If you peep over the parapet you would draw a bullet almost at once … One task that was always dangerous was fetching of rations and water. As you went along the trench every corner was a death trap … We had casualties every day. Sickness began to make inroads into our strength; every man that left us made more work for those that remained.

Like many others he finally also succumbed to disease, and suffering from an attack of dysentery he set off to the UK, noting as he did,

I shall always remember the hopeless dawns, the thirst, hunger, filthy heat, stench, and millions of green flies coming off the unburied corpses and settling on one's food, the sunken cheeks and the staring eyes of men dying.

The Yeomanry were not the only Worcestershire men at Gallipoli – the 4th Worcestershire battalion had embarked from England on 3 July 1915 and arrived in Lemnos on the 20th. Here they found there were no tents, and the sand was everywhere, causing everything to be very uncomfortable when the wind was up. Private John Barret kept a diary of the miserable experience.

After fighting in the trenches, which was 'too awful for thinking about', the battalion was back in the same trenches a week after. This time, they were 'in the firing line, the same line as where we made the charge from. The bodies of our late comrades still lay between the trenches'. Attempts to spend some time relaxing were fraught as well. Barrett described how his company 'went into village last night and two soldiers (one black) were locked up for being drunk. The village is put out of bounds and no beer can be obtained there only wine'.[10]

Back in Egypt after defence and training, moving back and forth between the camps at Kantara and Ismailia, the division joined the defence of the Suez Canal against the Turkish invasion of spring 1916.[11] In March 1917 they mounted a major offensive into Palestine against the Turks. The first and second battles of Gaza cost the British over 10,000 men. The British made slow and piecemeal headway during 1917, as Cyril Sladden described in letters he wrote home to his fiancé, with the news then conveyed on to his father:

There is no rest at all at this job. We have been having a series of moves each preceded as a rule by a little scrapping sometimes the Turk has stayed to be turned out; sometimes he had left the place vacant. But in either case the preparation and precautions are the same, and involve digging at high pressure at first and of course involving the best part of a night (or all of it) to make oneself reasonably safe and secure some convenience really takes about a week of steady hard work. For a space of 2 or 3 days in a new place one simply rubs along somehow. After 2 or 3 days we have been allowed to stop, the latest indications point to our being our first as insecure here where we thought we were really likely to be in a place of peace for a time.

It is very sickening work going from place to place never settling anywhere and always handing over to someone else the results of one's strenuous labours. Somehow we seemed to have handed it on, and I have kept on pushing out a ½ a mile or so at a time, first because we were the people on the spot who knew the ground. After establishing ourselves on ahead we were of course equally the people on the spot for the next push.

Our present location, could we only rest here, is pleasant enough. We are on the river again as the result of much pushing at the furthest point up stream which we hold to be near a river is to be near water, and that is always a great benefit even though snipers on the other side limit our means to enjoy it.

It has been the most extraordinary experience of open fighting, we have been disposed over wide stretches of country in manoeuvres that would make the hair of a tactical theorist stand on end.

Almost daily there is something doing somewhere and we are getting so used to the noise of the attacks within a few miles that we take comparatively small notice of them. Of course just before when and where they are to take place & generally a few hours afterwards whether or not they have been successful generally they have been but not always at the first attempt.

… Meanwhile I constantly congratulate myself on not being a Turk it must be a horrid existence [Later] during my interval for lunch we had news of a further attack again successful, a lot of Turks surrendering so apparently my last remark is justified!

[Later again] Great headlines in the papers will announce the Events that have happened today close to here. We have just been told of 2000 prisoners taken and more being brought in. It seems as if the head has been cleared today & the enemy cannot slip away in darkness as they have contrived to do before. Such good news and most cheering.[12]

As defeats, failures and lack of conclusions mounted up in France, some British politicians felt that the way to win the war was by increasing attention to other theatres, such as Gallipoli and the Middle East.[13] The relative military successes here, especially with the fall of Jerusalem late in 1917, led contemporary and subsequent commentators to feel vindicated in their views, and this has contributed to a rather more romantic idea of what war in the desert was like. The Arab revolt against the Turks, and especially the leadership of that revolt by a British officer, Colonel T. E. Lawrence – the Lawrence of Arabia so memorably reprised on screen by a dashing blue-eyed Peter O'Toole – has only reinforced that perspective.

Victor Godrich fully recovered by the end of 1916, and was again destined for the Middle East to take part in the first and second battles of Gaza, reaching Jerusalem in 1918. This time he travelled across France to Marseilles and then by French ship to arrive in Alexandria on 26 December. Continuing via train and horse his party joined the regiment at El Bitia, noting, 'They looked a thoroughly disreputable lot to us, who had come straight from the land of clean buttons.' Within two weeks of his arrival he was in battle on 9 January, and after a long day of fighting there were 500 British casualties, 3,000 prisoners and a twenty-five-mile march back to base.

I shall never forget that march – a gruelling day … we had all but reached the limit of human endurance. Practically everybody slept in the saddle and left it to the horse to get them home. The next day we had the Christmas free-issue of canteen goods out of the profits made by the canteen during the previous 12 months.

Victor moved to El Burj, was made up to lance corporal in February 1917 and was sent on a Hotchkiss gun training course in Cairo, before moving on to participate in the First Battle of Gaza and then on the 19 April 1917 in the Second Battle of Gaza.

We left our bivouacs at 2 am and marched until daybreak … I had a heavy load to labour under for I carried the Hotchkiss everywhere I went – we gunners were in great demand. The Turks allowed us to come well in range, then they let us have it … The 5.9 shells dropped several of our boys early on. I saw Joe Matthews in the next troop to ours killed, Bert Ricketts and Tom Nixon wounded. We pushed on and were soon within rifle range (about 1,000 yards). Lying on our faces for a breather, with bullets dropping all around us, we wondered whether we should ever live to get up to the Turkish trenches where we could plainly see the Turks firing at us …

I recollect a fat Turkish officer whom I dropped at about 400 yards. I can now see the light canvas uniforms with bright brass buttons and Turks firing at us from their hips as they advanced. We continued to fire whenever we could see one or two, but they did not come again … After collecting our dead and wounded, we retired about half a mile and waited for the horses – very glad THAT day was over.

The casualty list for that day was high, particularly among the Worcestershire infantry. Victor Godrich continued to be engaged in a number of smaller skirmishes, often travelling in the heat and dust storms. The conditions took their toll; ill with sunstroke and exhaustion he was sent for a couple of weeks to the rest camp in Marakeb in late June 1917. The following month the director of medical services lined the troops up for inspection in Marakeb.

It was really an eye opener to anyone new to the desert. Every man in the fighting forces was covered with septic sores on their hands, faces and legs – all in bandages. My own hands did not heal properly until December. All this trouble was no doubt due to the poor state of our blood.

If one's hand was accidentally knocked against the saddle, a large piece of skin came off. The result was an open sore that would not heal. The swarms of flies settling on the sore did not improve matters, so we had to use bandages for self-preservation.

Despite the misery and horror of war, illness and danger, there were also interludes of calm, leisure and relaxation for the Worcestershire soldiers in the Middle East when in the rest camps; they could eat in local restaurants and engage in football matches and other sporting activities, which were sometimes reported in the local Worcestershire newspapers, for example,

A very interesting match was played between the officers and the sergeants of the I/Ist Queen's Own Worcestershire Hussars, the scene of the contest being about 100 miles east of the Suez canal … In spite of the heavy going owing to the deep sand a very fast pace was kept up throughout the game, which ended in a win for the officers by 4 goals to 0.[14]

Sometimes there was scope for sightseeing, as Jack Preece described to his parents: 'The same morning Hal and I got permission to have a ride on our horses so we went to the pyramids and Sphinx. I should like Dad to see them they are fine sights.'[15] There was also of course the pleasure of bathing in a hot climate; the postcards soldiers sent to relatives and the photographs in the newspapers pay tribute to this. Between 12 May and 31 July Victor was based in Latron.

A group of machine gunners in Egypt, from *Berrows Worcestershire Journal*, 1918.

Postcard of Egyptian pyramids.

I have happy memories of Latron. Out food was plentiful and good, our regimental canteen was well stocked with all the extras that a man wants, the discipline was easy and the duties were light, In fact we almost forgot there was a war on. It was 90 degrees in the shade every day, there was nothing going on along the whole front of Palestine – operations commenced each year in September.

Like almost all other British soldiers of the First World War, Victor Godrich had had a Christian education and upbringing. With death and disease all around, on 19 October 1917 he recalled,

I was confirmed at Shellal by the Bishop of Jerusalem. The ceremony took place in a marquee erected for the occasion. There were about 200 received.

The Service was impressive, for all we knew the fighting was to commence shortly and realised that this might be the last Service that some of us would take part in. I took my first Communion the following Sunday in the little tent of our Brigade Chaplain.

An added problem to this group of the Yeomanry, who were frequently travelling in extreme heat, was that at times there was no ready supply of water. Victor recalled on one occasion that

we soon realised we were in a nasty place, apart from the bullets, for the only available water was at Beersheba (20 miles away). It was a case of self-denial with a vengeance.

A fearful thirst in your mouth, a pint of water in your bottle which was dangling on your chest and you have to keep saying to yourself, No, No, No, but towards midnight we were told that a water cart had arrived so went down with a load of bottles.

We were given another pint, which lasted us the next 24 hours (all through the following day under a merciless sun which makes the rocks so hot you could not touch them).

When we were not shooting at the Turks, we had some time to look around at the scenery; the most interesting view was to the north, which included Beersheba to Jerusalem road.

Several miles up this road, on a hill was a large Arab town, its white walls shining bright in the sun. We discovered later that this was the ancient city of Hebron, mentioned in the Bible several times.

Some of the places Victor saw in the Middle East would have been familiar from the Christian culture in which he had been educated, particularly when, as he put it, in April 1918 'we found ourselves riding through the suburbs of the famous city'.

Jerusalem has outgrown its old walls just like Gloucester, Chester, York and most of our own walled cities have done but the old city is still the heart and the core. We were surprised to see the wall in very good condition. After passing the tomb of the Virgin Mary and St Stephen, who was stoned to death at this spot, one can see on the hill above the road, the two buildings which mark the Garden of Gethsemane. The garden, or olive orchard as it no doubt was, extended all over the side of hill. So the Greek and Roman Churches have both walled off about an acre.

Each built a church and then claimed their own spot to be the actual site. No harm is done by this for nobody knows which is correct and the gardens are beautifully kept. A little incident occurred at this spot, which shows how callous and indifferent army life made a man. My pal Jack Mills was riding behind me, so knowing that Jack was a devout Catholic I said in a soft voice 'this is the Garden of Gethsemane on the left' Jack said 'oh is it' and resumed his chatter with this partner ...

Above the walls we could see Church towers, Minarets and other tall buildings but overshadowing them all was the green dome of the Mosque of Omar. It seems incongruous that the largest and stateliest building in the home of Christianity should be a Mohamedan Mosque, but that is history.

Victor Godrich remained in the Middle East until spring 1919 when he was transported back to Britain, arriving at Snow Hill Station on 6 April 1919.

Postcard collected by a Yeomanry soldiers in Egypt.

3

Agriculture and Food Production

When war broke out, Worcestershire was a predominantly rural county; as war progressed, its agriculture was an increasingly important part of its contributions to the war effort. Britain by the early twentieth century was far from self-sufficient in food; there was a heavy reliance on imports. For example, nearly 80 per cent of the grain consumed in Britain, used to make bread – the staple in the working-class diet – was imported from the USA. At the beginning of the war there was in retrospect what can be seen as an over-confident approach to food supplies. The *Worcester Daily News* was able to reassuringly report the Board of Agriculture's announcement that 'they could say with confidence that there is actually in the United Kingdom at the present time, including the home crop now being harvested, five months supply of breadstuffs'.[1] While the myth that people believed that the war would be over by Christmas has little foundation, there was not the realisation at this point that Britain was at the beginning of a four-year haul. Nor was there an understanding that cargo ships would be seen as legitimate targets of war and that naval blockades would make food supplies a key element of fighting the first 'total' war.

Consequently there were no restrictions on who was recruited into the army; agricultural labourers – due to poor wages, uncertainty of employment and employer pressure in some areas – seem to have been particularly susceptible to the call to the colours. In Pershore and the surrounding district alone, 1,000 men fought in the First World War. Significant numbers of horses were also either volunteered for war service by their owners or requisitioned. Yet the local newspapers echoed the central government's buoyant attitude in reporting the challenges that Worcestershire farmers faced in getting the 1914 harvest in. Despite the rain in early August, the corn had dried and they claimed that

here and there one hears of a serious shortage of horse labour but that will gradually be overcome as the harvest processes. Neighbours will lend a hand as they have done on other occasions. Should there be further call upon the rural horse reserves, immediately the problem would be more serious and assume national rather than local importance.[2]

But they also acknowledged on the same day that there had been many complaints, questioning the parity and fairness of the process of requisitioning horses. The harvest was successfully gathered in part due to the activities of some agricultural workers, who had signed up, popping home to assist as needed, much to the consternation of some of their peers. Not everyone shared the confidence of the government and the local papers. A well-attended meeting of the National Farmers Union in Upton on Severn on 11 September sought to petition the government to take action to safeguard wheat crops and suggested that there should be financial inducement to ensure the wider planning of wheat. Their suggestions and concerns were not heeded, although in many ways they were prophetic.[3]

Worcestershire's agriculture included the highest proportions of smallholdings in the country, nearly 3,000 of between one to five acres, with 75 per cent of its agriculture tied up in small farms under fifty acres; hence the county was described as the 'home of the smallholder'. A significant impetus to the development of these smallholdings was the 1908 Small Holdings and Allotments Act, which allowed county councils to buy up farms for sale and divide them up into smallholdings for rent. This was something Worcestershire County Council did with determination, taking over 50,000 acres. Such smallholdings were ideal for some crops, hops for example, but not for wheat. The intensively worked smallholdings usually relied upon family labour and involved growing a range of foodstuffs; fruit trees were sometimes underplanted with vegetables. Such small agricultural units were particularly hard hit when men went to war, and concern that fruit might go to waste led Fred Hall to write to the *Worcester Daily Times* in August 1914.

Sir – May I suggest that a portion of the Relief Fund collection be immediately used to purchase plums, apples and damsons to be bottled or made into jam. The Bank Street Soup Kitchen would make an excellent place to do the preserving and storing. Tons of fruit will not be picked and it will be an unpardonable offence if we permit the fruit to drop from the trees and decay. Farmers gladly accept a small price per pot. Ladies and gentlemen with motors, and other vehicles could convey pickers and assist in picking and many in the country will give every assistance. Get a small Committee of workers together and commence now the fruit is ready. You will have thousands of jam jars and bottles freely given.[4]

There were already established jam and canning factories in the Vale of Evesham, which was already famous and which meant that, at the outbreak of the First World War, Worcestershire already made a significant contribution to the total number of fruit and vegetables grown in Britain. There were a number of reasons for this. The geography of the area produced a climate and soil that was particularly suitable for these crops; protection from the Malvern, Bredon and Cotswold hills had a positive effect on the weather. Fruit often ripened up to a month before some neighbouring counties. Furthermore there were fourteen railway stations within five miles of Evesham, and as early as 1906 one of the leading local growers observed, 'We have an almost perfect train service to every part of the kingdom.'[5] Thus the fruit and vegetables from the area could be quickly transported to major towns such as Birmingham and Bristol. The smallholders were assisted by cooperative systems of marketing, such as the Littleton and Badsey Growers Association, which started in 1908.

The Worcestershire War Agricultural Executive Committee had overall responsibility for making agriculture more productive and efficient. One of the key problems would be ensuring an adequate supply of labour to the farms throughout the war to enable Worcestershire to play its part in increasing Britain's food supply. Agriculture was not particularly well mechanised; there were few tractors and a heavy reliance on horses in the Edwardian era. So another task of the committee was to coordinate the loans of horses, tractors and other machinery across all the farms and encourage greater mechanisation.

Farmers were initially encouraged and then instructed to shift their farming from animal husbandry to wheat production where possible, and non-productive land such as Defford Common was also ploughed up to grow wheat. The CWAC monitored the efficiency of farms, in time telling them what to plough and how to plough and fining those farmers who did not comply. Its role was increasingly seen by many farmers as intrusive; the frustration of the farmers can be seen in the following letter,

An image of Eros, an attachment for a Ford car to enable it to become a sort of tractor. From *Berrows Worcestershire Journal*.

although with its original punctuation it is not always easy to follow.

July 9th 1915

To Mr. Lauder F.S.T

Dear Sir in reply to your letter of the 9th inst[ance] re my cattle on the common I have homed my cattle on the farm let to me but please <u>note</u> I understand they have been in attendance always by my <u>son</u> & <u>daughter</u> or myself on a Sunday but always weekdays by the children and that has only been for an hour in the morning before commencing school and for about 2 hours of an evening after I <u>have</u> milked them but never unattended you <u>understand</u> and those persons that can prove this statement to be untrue I shall be most pleased to meet them any time to prove it right and who ever the party concerned may be that informed you that my cattle has been on the wheat planted by the Committee & damaged it told you a very great untruth as I should be <u>very very</u> <u>sorry</u> to have such a thing happen as wheat is not a good thing for cattle to eat as it would do them great harm so I should be rather a foolish man to let them eat it will you ask Mr. Backhouse & the day master of the farm that if they have ever seen my cattle on the wheat or if unattended or not they spoke to my two children last week last friday evening after they had called here and said are you minding the cattle they replied yes sir as they came back up through my fields into the common ask them also or Major Hill if they have ever seen any sheep on it at any time I am afraid their reply will be yes only last week the soldier told me himself he put those lot of sheep off 3 times one day last week now some good samaritan wants to put it onto my cattle that has done the damage if any done do you consider this a right thing for a person to write such an untruth about a mans cattle Will you kindly inform who the person may be and I will make them prove it I like the truth about a thing the committee themselves and all other labor that has been here have inquired off my wife or self whose sheep those are lots of times now if my cattle that has done it. It is quite impossible for me to erect a fence yet as the ground is dry and I could not drive stakes in far enough as they would brake as the ground is so dry and hard until we can get rain it will give me great pleasure if you will send me the person or persons named in this to satisfy my rights over such a matter

yours obligingly F.H.[6]

P.S. I do not see why my cattle could not go on the lot let to me when in attendance always

This letter also draws attention to role that children played in food production. They helped on smallholdings and small family farms. Children replaced elder siblings or fathers who had gone to war, assisting their mothers, many of whom found themselves with the sole responsibility for maintaining the smallholding when their husbands joined the armed forces. The *Worcester Herald* contained a number of articles and letters concerning the labour scarcity in Kidderminster, for example with suggestions for greater use of child labour and arguments that those children who were not very intellectually inclined should be allowed to leave school early to undertake agricultural work.[7] This was a position supported by the National Farmers Union, which urged the more widespread use of child labour in Worcestershire.[8]

Worcestershire become the third-highest users of child labour in agriculture in the country during the war, and the fruit-growing town of Pershore was one of the highest employers of children within Worcestershire. The trend towards child labour began as soon as war started on 11 August 1914; it was reported that four Scouts had been sent to Pershore to help with fruit picking as the war had taken away so many men on the fruit plantations. Children continued to provide seasonal labour, gathering in harvests throughout the war, although they were not permitted in the hop fields unaccompanied by their parents below the age of seven. Children often retained a sense of mischief despite their work, as with a case involving two young boys aged eleven and thirteen, who were charged with throwing potatoes at a passing motor car while they were potato digging. Apparently large numbers of potatoes were thrown and a potato struck one of the passengers. The boys were discharged with a caution.[9]

Notwithstanding the tensions created by governmental interference in the first few months of the war, things went relatively well for agriculture. There was a strong demand for produce, assisted by the military's need to purchase food supplies on which to feed the British and Allied soldiers, at home and at the front. There was encouragement to grow more sugar beet, particularly around Kidderminster. However, the increased purchase tax on beer and the reduced opening hours for pubs cast a shadow over the hop-growing industry's long-term survival.[10]

A degree of optimism was also expressed by Lord Coventry in 1915 in a letter published in *Country Life* magazine when he says,

I imagine farming will go on pretty much as it does at present, though I dare say the difficulty of procuring good labour will be increased. At present prices all round for corn, hay straw, horses and livestock of every description are satisfactory and these pries will probably be maintained for some time to come. But there is another side of the picture, and people must not run away with the idea that famers are enjoying unalloyed prosperity. Thus those who are buyers not breeders will find a difficulty in buying livestock even at a high price; feeding stuffs are dear; labour is scarce, and rates are high. Nevertheless I am inclined to think – as I hope – that tenant farmers will be able to hold their own.[11]

He went on to articulate his concerns that rates, taxes and tithes and subscriptions would eat up landowners' profits; for many of them it was death duties to be paid when their owners died in war that became a problem. Approximately 20 per cent of Britain's large estates had to be sold in the 1920s. In 1915 Lord Coventry's concern about procuring good labour is echoed across many areas of the local press, the *Worcester Herald* noting the following month the shortage of men to pick fruit and hops.[12] The *Birmingham Evening Post* noted that in Worcestershire not only was the drought a problem in 1915, but that

farmers are handicapped severely by the scarcity of labourers and applications are being made in the headquarters of the Worcestershire Regiment for the soldiers to assist during hay and corn harvest season. A large area of arable land has not been planted at all. In one district over one hundred acres are lying idle through inability to get labour at the right planting season. Female labour has been introduced in all branches of farming work but the supply is altogether inadequate to meet the demand.[13]

In the pre-war era most of the women who worked on the land did so as part of their husband's employment, in family farms or temporarily at harvest time. Many of the 'village women' who might have been expected to be drawn into agricultural work in wartime seem to have been resistant. Perhaps this was because for the previous fifty years women had been encouraged to think that agricultural work was inappropriate for them. It was certainly frowned upon by many in the Edwardian period, when women were not commonly seen in the fields in Worcestershire. A public meeting held under the auspices of the Worcestershire War Agricultural Executive Committee at the church institute in Malvern Wells discussed the need to get women onto the land in September 1915. Mr James Woodyatt, Chairman of the Malvern Urban District Council Sub-Committee, argued that

every effort must be made to increase the production of food ... Men were wanted for the Army and at the same time farmers and others were asked to secure the maximum production from the land. He thought the strain upon the farmers would get heavier as time went on and that difficulties in labour supplies and transport would increase until peace was declared. Many of those who came under the category of 'the idle rich' should be asked to work. These were no days for snobbery, honest labour was no disgrace to a man or women and an expert workman was an honour to his country. Any gentleman or lady, whatever their position, who did a day's work on the land ought to be paid. If they did not make use of the money then there were many charitable institutions in need of assistance. He did not think the farmer should get gratuitous labour. If a woman did man's work she ought to receive a man's wages. By increasing the production of food money would be kept in the county.[14]

Woodyatt's arguments reflected some of the discussions that emerged as lighter agricultural work – such as dairying, poultry keeping and horticulture – had begun to appeal to middle-class and urban women in wartime. The Women's Farm and Garden Union had many college-educated women and they assisted in organising the Women's Land National Service Corps. Some of these women saw themselves as working in a supervisory capacity to 'educate' local village women, and were in danger of alienating working-class women. Some students, however, spent their summer holidays choosing to work alongside regular fruit pickers, as this young woman explains:

The party which set out for work was a strange sight to see; our attire was a marvellous motley – old waterproofs, mackintosh skirts, hockey leggings, old hats, bathing caps, sun-bonnets, motor-coats, hurden aprons – anything old which would keep out the wet. One enterprising lady wore her father's boots over her own. We were usually laden with sacks and buckets to pick into, baskets of bread and cheese and bottles of water. Our bedraggled appearance on our return home after a wet day was even more entertaining, and proved a festival for the village children.

Our work was of various kinds – pea-picking, bean-picking, plum-picking, thistle-cutting, bean topping, and for the last week harvest work. Plum-picking proves exciting at times, when two ladders locked together over a tree begin to slip, and the pickers clasp hands in terror, gazing with agony into each other's eyes, waiting for the end – which is fortunately averted by the interposition of a lower branch. Bean-picking work occupied most of the time; it was back-breaking work, and three weeks of it seems now impossible to contemplate. At the end of our last day's bean-picking one of the party solemnly plucked a bean-flower, and ground it into the earth with her heel, as a declaration of our heart-felt detestation of dwarf kidney-beans. Harvest-work was the heaviest, but by far the most interesting of all the kinds of work we tried. Largely because we felt it to be more vitally important than the other work, we were, one and all, extremely enthusiastic over it.[15]

There appears to have been resistance by some farmers to employing women workers, or, perhaps more accurately, to employing women who were not family members. There was also resistance from trade unionists who were concerned the employment of women would undercut the already low wages of agricultural workers, which Woodyatt addressed by suggesting that a woman who did a man's work should get a man's pay. However, the management of the horses, ploughing, scything etc. were considered highly skilled (and male) occupations which it was felt women could not do.

Group of women war workers on Lord Hindlip's Estate, 1917. From *Berrows Worcestershire Journal*.

Others at the Malvern meeting suggested women could rear calves and attend to lambs, and as spring advanced there would be plenty of field work such as light hoeing and thistle cutting. There was, however, a degree of concern expressed about the welfare of children while mothers worked. Some mothers, it appeared, were criticised for not wanting to leave their children, others for being too willing to do so, and suggestions were made for crèches and nurseries to be set up with the support of the Board of Education. Others suggested laundries should be provided to undertake the children's washing. (However, no evidence that this occurred has as yet been found.) A Mr Allsebrook gave the Board of Agriculture's perspective:

It was a matter of great urgency that we should produce more food in this country, and so retain money to pay for other things we had to import such as the munitions of war. The chief difficulty that confronted agriculture was the question of labour and he was afraid the labourer's wives and daughters had not realised the extreme need of help, Going about the country, as he did, he could not help seeing the state in which the land had got for want of labour. What would be the position a year hence if we did not grapple with the problem.[16]

In 1916 the Worcestershire War Agricultural Executive Committee set up a Women's War Agricultural Committee, with one of its main aims to try to encourage and to register women prepared to work on the land. Women who completed thirty days' approved service received an armband and a certificate which explained, 'Every woman who helps in agriculture during the war is serving her country as the man who is fighting in the trenches or on the sea,' signed by the President of the Board of Agriculture. A large public meeting was held at Shirehall in Worcestershire on 1 March 1916 with Mr F. D. Acland from the Board of Agriculture and Lord Coventry of Croome Court attempting to encourage the greater employment of women in agriculture in Worcestershire, even if only for short periods over the summer. A Birmingham University student describes her experience at Elmley Castle:

Looking back on six weeks of war-work at Elmley Castle our memories seem to be bounded – and blurred – by vistas and vistas of green. What? you ask. Green peas! For we picked peas of all varieties and peas in all directions – in Elmley itself, at Fladbury, Cropthorne, Wick, and Evesham … We occasionally got variations from pea-picking – gathering raspberries, blackcurrants, broad and kidney beans. But were we not glad to get back to old friends, the peas! – especially after those fearful broad beans. If you ever see a field of really hefty, tough, long-since-mature broad beans, work not in that field if you are wise. In order to save labour we had to uproot the bean-plants, and after struggling valiantly with these awful monsters we returned covered with honourable but painful scars and blisters, and groaning under sundry aches and stiffnesses.

Only once did we have time to see how truly picturesque was the field in which we were working. On the last day of all, two of us did 'day work', pulling seed-peas and hoeing. Day-work is much less strenuous than piece-work, and curious little sidelight on human nature – it was most noticeable that the quickest piece-workers were the most appalling slackers when on day-work. We enjoyed that last day partly because we got to know the 'regular' women really well, for we joined them in building up a huge camp fire, whose smoke made the boughs of the giant tree above dance riotously, and also because the wide twenty-acre field was a glorious medley of colour …

We also became involved in Labour problems, and took part in a strike for more wages – again for picking peas. For some days, a company of 'travellers' – tramps of the caravan-dwelling persuasion – had settled on a field of peas which were ready for picking. They were becoming somewhat restive, as for two days the overseers had not arrived and also because they had been offered 7*d.* per pot for peas which were 'bad picking', and there seems to exist an unwritten law to the effect that 'the worse the picking, the higher the wage'. On this eventful morning the overseers had arrived, but no-one would work, as the would-be employers still offered 7*d*. and the prospective employees demanded 9*d*. Finally, with a large concourse of travellers listening and watching outside, and feeling as though the fate of a nation were trembling in the balance, I entered into diplomatic relations with the employer over the telephone, and, as usually happens, we ended with a compromise, and at 8*d*. per pot we all set to work.

Though our work was strenuous and the hours long, Elmley has other memories besides those of toil and stress. Rides to work in the cool delicious air of early summer mornings and plunges into the Avon after a hot and tiring day compensated for many ills. Being made wise by experience, we endeavoured always to get to the field before the sun got high and while the dew still lay on the grass. Once, when we rose at 4.30 a.m., after being roused by our next-door neighbour beating a tattoo with a long pole on the windows, we even caught glimpses of faint stars still shining in the sky. And of all memories of Elmley, that of Bredon Hill is best of all. Bredon – the Bredon of a 'Shropshire Lad' – is a storehouse of wonders. Elmely village lies at the foot of its thyme-clad slopes ...[17]

The introduction of conscription in 1916, initially for single men and then extended to those who were married, made the labour situation considerably worse for agriculture in Worcestershire. The military tribunals heard many appeals against conscription from agricultural workers (often on family farms and smallholdings); some were for exemption for military service entirely and many requested delays of a month or two in order to get affairs in order, to plant or harvest a particular crop or to train someone to do their job. Delays were often treated sympathetically, but the idea that agriculture was vital war work and therefore exempted men from fighting was not, as the following newspaper report makes clear:

With regard to the statement in the Press that the Military Representative at Preston had recovered a telegram from the War

Office that no more men engaged on the land were to be called pending further instruction. Major G. H. Smith the Recruiting Officer for the Worcester District says that this is not a standing order, but only a temporary suspension made doubtless, with the view of dealing with the question of substitution of labour and position of agriculture generally. He said in every case where they could offer a farmer another man they would do so and apply to have the exception cancelled. Meanwhile Tribunals were quite right in dealing with the cases on their merits and leaving the question of calling-up to the Military, Major Smith added that general service men, if excepted at all, ought to be given only temporary certificates in order that the substitution scheme might operate and further temporary exceptions ought to be given only in cases where the man was absolutely indispensible.[18]

The situation became more severe in 1917 when Worcestershire was required not only to maintain its fruit and vegetable cultivation but also bring a further 40,000 acres into the cultivation of corn. Farmers who failed to comply with instructions from the committee to plough wheat could face tough fines; this and the price restrictions on many of the crops that farmers sold resulted in voices of discontent at many of the meetings of the National Farmers' Union.[19] There was close co-operation between the Worcestershire War Agricultural Executive Committee and the Military Tribunals, especially around the use of soldiers for agricultural work. On March 10 1917 the committee advertised to farmers that they had

125 MEN

Fit, able-bodied (30 of whom are horsemen or
ploughmen) available until 16 April also

180 MEN

Able-bodied (some with agricultural experience)
available (unless urgent military reasons
prevent) until the end of the war.

The chair of the Worcestershire War Agricultural Executive Committee sat on the tribunal and the committee monitored the actions of those who had been granted exemption and reported those who they considered were not working according to their exemption certificates. Tribunals seem to have become harsher as the war progressed and at the tribunal on the 5 May 1918, of the thirty-nine young men between the ages of nineteen and twenty-three who applied for exception it was granted to only four.

Other strategies to address the shortfall of agricultural labour included using: those below and above conscription age, gangs of German prisoners of war, Belgian refugees, soldiers no longer fit for service, Irish labourers and students. Children from Worcestershire schools also played their part by participating in the great blackberry pick, competing with other counties to see who could collect the most blackberries to make into jam to go to feed soldiers at the front.

The official Women's Land Army was formed in 1917 by Roland Prothero, President of the Board of Agriculture. Although there are different figures, there seem to have been between 11,000 and 20,000 in the Land Army across the country, although over a quarter of a million women worked in agriculture during the war. The Land Army operated from 1917 to November 1919 and indeed women were still being directed towards the WLA after

Girls from British School, Worcester, ready to go blackberry picking in 1917. From *Berrows Worcestershire Journal*.

the war ended. Significantly, those in the Land Army could be shifted around the county. They did have training, uniform and a wage of 18s to 20s, which was not equal to a male agricultural worker's wage but was close to it. They could get extra payments if the skills they had, for example in ploughing or tractor driving, were recognised.

A temporary member of the Women's Land Army describes her experience:

After much complicated correspondence with certain unknown persons in London, and the payment of three shillings and sixpence, we at length became members of the Women's Land Army and were forwarded khaki armlets to prove the fact. Shortly afterwards we received various typewritten documents giving most attractive accounts of camps organised for our benefit, and finally we were ordered to proceed to Pershore to join a camp there.

We arrived late one Saturday afternoon at Pershore Station, all wearing our armlets according to orders. Here we fell in with about

Land Girls by a caravan in Stoke Heath. From *Berrows Worcestershire Journal*.

two-dozen Irish girls who had come from Belfast to work at the same farm. Two Land Army workers met us; we recognised them by their sunburnt laces and their armlets – armlets in a very different condition from ours, for already their wearers had been six weeks on the land, and the purple triangle with which each armlet was adorned was bleached almost white with the sun, and the whole affair showed signs of wear.

Our abode for the next six weeks was to be a stable, but no ordinary stable – it was as one of our party described it, 'a perfectly heavenly stable'. The farm hands had been hard at work and had thoroughly whitewashed the whole. The boxes were filled with clean, fresh straw, and altogether the whole place looked very inviting.

We began work at six each morning. The first day we were put on strawberries. Fortunately the patch was very small, and by twelve o'clock we had finished. Then we were sent down to the cabbage patch to 'fetch out the fat hens'. We had visions of something in the poultry line, but soon found the 'fat hen' to be a weed, quite easy to pull up. After dinner six of us were put hoeing in the blackcurrant patch, 'real 'eavy 'oeing', as one of our farm friends described it; but we had a fine view of Bredon, so what did it matter?

We picked raspberries for six weeks, with a few brief interludes of currant, loganberry, and strawberry picking. Wet or fine, we picked, until raspberries came and sat by our beds and haunted our dreams. The stable re-echoed at night to the sound of an Irish voice begging for more punnets (this was our record picker, who always filled a dozen punnets in record time); and another sleeper made the night hideous by continually calling to Harry, our foreman, to find her a new row.

Life in camp was very interesting. At the height of the picking season we numbered thirty-six; twenty-four had their quarters in the stable, and twelve in the loft. All our meals, which were cooked and prepared for us by our Captain and her Orderly, were served in the barn. It was a great relief to have no responsibility in that direction.

We had many a jolly sing-song in the barn with the piano, and, in fact, had quite good concerts at times. 'The powers that be' from the Land Army Council paid two visits of inspection to our camp. The second time they came we had been picking blackcurrants all afternoon in the rain, and were objects delightful to behold. The visitors arrived during this downpour, and were in time to share in a specially 'posh' tea, given in honour of the Irish party, who were leaving next day. After tea we arranged an impromptu concert. We had several good singers, a violinist, and a little Irish girl who recited charmingly. Various reverend gentlemen made speeches.[20]

The tea party indicates the social recognition given to those in various government schemes to get women onto the land. Land girls, although they were not numerous, became an icon of women's participation in the war effort and they took part in parades and appeared on posters and in other propaganda.

Dressed in their white smocks, seen in the sun-soaked countryside with small animals, they were a comforting image of war. But the WLA was hard work as Rowland Prothero, President of the Board of Agriculture also pointed out to the commons in 1918.

Physically the work is hard. It is monotonous. It is carried on out-of-doors in all conditions of weather, and in respect of accommodation

The Land Army on parade in Worcester, 1918. From *Berrows Worcestershire Journal*.

it implies real privation and real hardship. These facts have never been concealed; yet we have got, or we had at the end of the financial year – the numbers are larger now – 11,000 women who had patriotically responded to the appeal. That appeal is strengthened, I think, by the fact that they have to make sacrifices, and have to endure privations, which to some extent are comparable to those of their friends and relations at the front. Certain inducements we do offer. We give a month's training free. I know you cannot call it real training, it is more to get their muscles into something like condition, to give them something approaching the condition required for agricultural work.[21]

Prisoners of war, unless they were officers, were required to undertake work, and they too were seen as a potential answer to Worcestershire's shortage of agricultural labour. The Worcestershire War Agricultural Executive Committee and the local military assessed potential sites for tented camps for German POWs. They were not keen for them to be near schools, but placed three at Hampton House and Badsey Manor House and then Craycombe so that by the summer of 1918 there were 500 German POWs working on the land around Evesham. The market gardeners of Evesham Vale preferred the use of POWs to conscientious objectors, who they were not prepared to employ. The POWs were initially often expected to do the harder unskilled physical work, dredging ditches and working in gangs accompanied by guards. Things became more relaxed in time, with groups of prisoners dropped off on farms to work for the day. They seem to have got on well with the local communities, although farmers supplying them with cider and cigarettes was not approved of, nor was the extremely friendly greetings they received from local young women. Indeed, Colonel Wheeler remarked that 'the way in which the prisoners were being treated by young girls and other people throughout the country waving and communicating with them showed that people did not realize how our prisoners were being treated in Germany'. The controversy over POWs did not end with the friendliness of the local community as the food crisis increased in 1918. The *Evesham Journal* felt it necessary to provide frequent updates on the prisoners' rations, pointing out that when 'they were not working their maize meal and bread rations were reduced', and at a public meeting the local food commissioner in Evesham proposed he was going to stop supplying the German POWs with either beef or mutton and substitute horse meat.[22]

Thus a medley of individuals, from POWs to students, children to Land Army women and Irish labourers to travellers ensured that the fruit harvests of the Vale of Evesham were collected. Plums were just one of the many fruits that were harvested in the Vale of Evesham prior to the First World War, and the two varieties of Pershore plum became particularly important during the war because they leant themselves so well to fruit preservation. Both were developed at the end of the nineteenth and in the early twentieth century, by grafting trees growing in the ancient Tiddesley woods. The yellow, larger Pershore plum was particularly good for jam making and the Pershore Purple was a small, tart plum ideal for bottling, canning and pickling. Bottled plums replaced prunes, which were no longer being imported, while jam was eaten by urban working classes and soldiers alike on bread. Plums were also used in cakes tarts, pies (both sweet and savoury) and puddings, including plum pudding eaten at Christmas.

In 1918 there was nationally a very poor plum harvest; Pershore and Evesham district was one of the few parts of England where plums could be found in what was a national shortage of the fruit. For the growers this caused some problems, as the Ministry of Food's cap on the price that could be charged for plums caused hardship to the growers while some jam manufacturers were seen to be making significant profits. This touched what was a raw nerve in wartime. The matter was raised in a House of Lords debate. In 1927 an aging Great

Western Locomotive was renamed the *Pershore Plum* at the request of the Worcester Branch of the National Farmers Union, commemorating the contribution of the fruit to wartime food production.

4

Women in Wartime

Women's experience of war was varied and influenced by class, age, marital status, whether they were urban or rural dwellers and multitude of other factors. For some young and single women the war offered an interesting range of new opportunities in their working, leisure and domestic lives. For example, when it became unacceptable for young, healthy men to be playing football while other men were on the battlefield, women's football became very popular, drawing good crowds and being reported in the local newspapers.

The Women's Land Army, which was discussed in chapter 3, and the munitions workers, who will be referred to in chapter 7, are familiar images of women in the First World War. The number of women in paid employment did increase during the conflict; however, the vast majority of women remained in the home and retained and extended their domestic roles and responsibilities. Consequently this chapter's focus is on Worcestershire housewives, the organisations they joined, the charitable work they did and their struggle for survival as war progressed and food shortages became more severe. War did little to change these women's position in society.

The outbreak of war produced a quandary for many middle-class and wealthy women, uncertain what their role should be during the conflict. The *Worcester Herald* was quick, however, to make suggestions:

Now that the dreaded hour has arrived and our country has been asked to take its part in the terrible war which may devastate Europe, we women have to think how we can best aid our soldiers at the front

A picture of a ladies' football match. From *Berrows Worcestershire Journal*, 1917.

and their families at home, there is much we can do and there are some things which we should certainly refrain from doing.

One of the most important of the latter duties is not to let our housekeeping desire to secure food at reasonable cost imperil the situation of others, perhaps less able than us to stand the strain of high prices. It seems to me against all principles of patriotism and citizenship to try to secure stores of food just at a time when we should be willing to make sacrifices for those less able than we are to buy in an advanced market. If war means some diminution of luxury for the well to do, it means starvation for the poor and to create by our selfishness an unnecessary run on food stuffs is to play into the hands of the unprincipled speculator.

We are told there is an adequate food supply and that panic is to be avoided by reasonable action and consideration for others. But even if there was a great rise surely the people who are now rushing to fill their store cupboards and larders are the very ones who must think how very much worse it must be for the poor who have a daily struggle to feed themselves and their children. Perhaps much of this rush for food has been due to want of thought but once it is brought before them will return to ... more worthy methods.

I heard that two or three grocers in our city had to close their doors to those inconsiderate customers on Wednesday, and this means that as they are unable at once to secure fresh supplies in consequence of the congestion of traffic prices are forced up beyond real necessity. If we cannot be a law unto ourselves it is to be hoped that the government will deal quickly with this matter and allow a certain amount of food to be purchased by individuals.[1]

Their concerns over food and housekeeping were increasingly justified as the war progressed. Even in the first week of the war, panic buying led to a sharp escalation of prices in many shops, and the *Worcester Herald* carried a story of a food riot in Bermondsey alongside its guidance on women's wartime role. Women were encouraged to undertake charitable work of various sorts, extending their domestic and caring roles beyond their homes and particularly extending care to the men in the armed forces and their families. The *Worcester Herald* continued,

There are however many other ways in which women can give material help at the present moment. I know that the Mayoress and Lady Hindlip, who is vice president for Worcester and the neighbourhood are considering various matters in relation to work to be taken in hand at once by members of the Red Cross Society: in connection with the supply of ambulance necessities and also the society for the relief of the wives and children of our soldiers and sailors. It would be well I think at the present for all branch societies formed for the relief of those engaged in war to join forces and co-operate in a well organised scheme so as to avoid overlapping and any waste of energy ...

There are clothes to be made for the men going into active service. I understand that flannel shirts are needed and that they must be cut and made in readiness. However these are only suggestions and the first thing to ascertain will be how many are able to answer the call for to be of real use we must get to work at once.[2]

The euphemism that men went to war and women knitted may be a little harsh, but in the first weeks of the war the *Worcester Daily Times* certainly contained a number of accounts of women of Worcestershire grouping together and busily knitting and sewing. As early as 10 August Droitwich had a sewing meeting; an appeal to women by the mayor and mayoress apparently resulted in 'the Town Hall being filled with ladies on Saturday afternoon making garments for soldiers at the front as well as bandages'[3] and other necessities. Meanwhile it was reported that in Upton-upon-Seven,

the ladies of the district are anxious to do their part, and work parties are being held at the Rectory to make useful garments for the sailors and soldiers at the front. The money needed to purchase the sewing material was easily raised in the town and district, many promising to give more if required.[4]

One middle-class housewife organised twice-weekly meetings in her home to make garments for soldiers.[5] Such activities took place alongside a general trend, emerging over the course of the war, for more centralised organisational structures to take over from ad hoc volunteerism. Many considered this necessary to avoid repetition and waste, which might occur if individuals were left to their own devices when undertaking patriotic work. Organisation and co-ordination was apparently required, hence in Worcester on 11 December 1914 the mayoress arranged a comfort day for the soldiers, which would centralise and prioritise activities around the provision of mittens. A local newspaper explained that this was

a special effort to provide the 3,000 soldiers now in Worcester with much-needed woollen mittens and mufflers. Tomorrow (Saturday) is the day appointed, and the Mayoress begs for contributions in at the Guildhall on that day. By ordering a very large number of mittens they can be procured at 1s and 1d a pair so that everyone giving this sum can ensure one of our local soldiers having warm hands, and any multiple of this amount they will be used in like manner. If however, people prefer to buy or make mittens then they will be gratefully received.[6]

In Worcester, examples of such charitable activities continued throughout the war. There was the Lady Mayoress's charity to help servicemen's wives and local residents set up in 1914; in 1916 there was a Christmas party organised for children orphaned by the war and also one provided for the wives and families of troops stationed at the Norton barracks.

Whist drives, garden fetes, Red Cross weeks, fundraising theatrical events, musical shows for prisoners of war and the Prince of Wales Appeal for Those in Distress: all provided opportunities for women to get involved in the war effort. This was something that particularly appealed to those whose organisational skills had been honed by the suffrage campaigns in Edwardian Britain.

Women's motivation to undertake charitable work was varied; for some it was about fulfilling their patriotic duty, feeling useful and doing something which connected them to their loved ones, while for others it was a way to deal with grief and loneliness and

A whist drive in 1916. From *Berrows Worcestershire Journal*.

Red Cross Week in 1917. From *Berrows Worcestershire Journal*.

obtain companionship. Thus women's organisations thrived in wartime Worcestershire. Some, such as the Women's Co-operative Guild, had been formed in the nineteenth century; others, such as the Women's Institute, were new. Patriotic charitable wartime activities and membership of women's organisations provided leisure and communality, a female space for the exchange of gossip and chatter, as the following description of a Women's Co-op Guild meeting makes clear:

On Wednesday evening the opening social of the Co-operative Guild was held at the Co-operative Hall. The president welcomed all the old and new members. The programme opened with the National

Anthem and between the dances the following musical items were given – Sung "Boys in Khaki, Boys in Blue". There were about 100 present and an enjoyable evening was spent.[7]

Women's suffrage societies had generally dissipated or been suspended in the first months of the war. However, Mrs Fawcett, the leader of the largest non-militant organisation – the National Union of Suffrage Societies – visited Worcester in 1915 to encourage women to undertake charitable and welfare work for the duration of the war. In a letter to the editor of the *Worcester Daily Times* the organising secretary explained the organisation's position:

SUFFRAGISTS SEEK SERVICE

Dear Sir – the National Union of Women's Suffrage Societies wishes it to be known that it has suspended its ordinary political work for the time being and is preparing to use the entire organisation of the Union for the help of those who will be the sufferers from the economic and industrial dislocations caused by the war. The Societies of the National Union throughout the country will be authorised to offer their kind service to the Local Authorities of every area and assist in any scheme for the relief of unemployment and distress which may be found necessary, and Mrs Moore Ede, the President of the Worcester Society, has informed the Mayor of Worcester that her Committee is prepared to place their services at the disposal of any Committee which he may call together for the purpose. All who are willing to volunteer for personal service of any kind are asked to communicate as soon as possible with the Organising Secretary, Miss J House, c/o Mrs Wilson, 14, The College from whom all further information may be obtained.[8]

For some middle-class women, particularly those who had been involved with the militant Women's Social and Political Union (smashing windows and burning post boxes, for example), charity and welfare seemed a little tame. In 1914 Eveline Haverfield founded the Women's Emergency Corps, which quickly became the Women's Voluntary Corps, and J. Lessingham Spreckley was asked to organise a branch in Worcester and its immediate neighbourhood. The precise intended role of the group remains a little unclear; in her letter to the *Worcester Herald* Spreckley suggested that it was 'to organise a disciplined body of women to be used in emergency for home defence by setting free as many able bodied as possible for active service; also to prevent the indiscriminate use of firearms by untrained women'.[9] In practice they undertook a range of voluntary work including cooking, running canteens, playing a role as interpreters, caring for mothers and babies, collecting and distributing, clothes care and driving horses and motor cars. Some were recruited for activities abroad.

A meeting at the Worcester Guildhall in November 1914 was so well attended that it had to be adjourned from a committee room to the council chamber. It was explained that the organisation would recruit women of between the ages of eighteen and forty who would get fit, drill and also cultivate among women the virtue of sacrifice for their country. To promote comradeship they adopted a uniform, as it was explained, 'If some were better dressed than others there would always be a class distinction which they were anxious to avoid. By wearing a uniform they would be placed on the same footing. The price of the uniform would not be prohibitive and might be paid for in instalments. The only other initial expense was 1*s* (5p) to be paid on enlistment and about ½*d* for each drill.'[10] The uniform actually had a total cost of £2, more than twice the weekly wage that many families were struggling to live on, hence the group recruited predominantly from the wealthier classes. A report of the meeting in the *Worcester Daily News* produced a flurry of letters, indicative of anxiety about women's position in wartime.

TO THE EDITOR
WOMEN'S VOLUNTARY RESERVE
Dear Sir – I was very interested to read in your issue of the 26th, an account of a meeting of the above organization.

While fully sympathizing with the desire of women to serve their country in every possible way during the crisis through which England is passing, I question strongly whether the best way to achieve this end is for women to enter actively the great military movement which is now of necessity sweeping the country.

In the first place women are classed by International law as non-combatants and can therefore be shot at sight if seen carrying arms. As long as this law is in existence, I cannot see that the Government are in a position to accept the services of the proposed organization.

Secondly as we are thus placed outside that fighting force of the nation; does not our work lie in the direction of educating public opinion on the possibility of achieving, when this awful war is over, a lasting peace.

Much as our gallant men suffer in time of war, the greatest sufferers are the women who by the very inaction that is laid upon them suffer mentally and physically. The symbolic figure of peace is a woman, this symbolizing cannot be transferred into fact if woman who is the fore-destined champion of peace, enters the ranks of war. The woman's part is then the hardest part, but I am convinced upon her shoulders to a very large extent is the answer to the question: 'Shall there be peace or war in the future?'

Whilst doing all in our power to bring this awful war to a successful end, let women band together not as a force for war, but as a force to prevent the awful repetition of the horrors we are now facing.

M. M. Williams.[11]

For others it was the uniform that appalled them most. There was a widespread enthusiasm for wearing uniform in the era, even by those who did not have the remotest chance of fighting. In a letter prefiguring the 1916 National War Savings Committee slogan that 'to dress extravagantly in wartime is worse than bad form it is unpatriotic', a member of one of the non-militant law-abiding suffragist organisations explained her criticism of the Women's Emergency Corps.

Sir – The Government are urging us all to be economical. The latest movement to improve the importance of the economy is that promoted by a number of distinguished ladies who ask members of their sex to give a pledge 'to buy as few luxuries as possible'. Cannot these ladies induce members of the Women's Emergency Corps to pay some regard to this one question? Our men volunteers (who, one imagines, will be made use of before the women are called upon to any extent) can manage to train and drill without uniform, but the women encourage each other to spend money on a uniform; which is not indispensable. I know of no duties that they are doing which cannot be done as well in ordinary dress as uniform. Not even those members with ample means ought to spare money to buy uniform in this crisis; but when one hears of young girls (in one case a servant) getting a few pounds a year advised to equip themselves in uniform (which is costly out of all proportion to their small means) there seems to be reason for protest. The greatest service the women can do for us at the present time is to refrain from consuming labour: and to cease trying to look impressive or picturesque.

SUFFRAGIST[12]

Most women had neither the time nor the money for such activities; their lives were shaped by domestic responsibilities and domestic caring roles, which in wartime were stretched to include not only a range of charitable activities but also looking after others in their homes, for example homeless Belgium refugees. Furthermore, as Worcestershire was a county with a strong military tradition, the recruitment and training of volunteers put a particular strain on homes in the area as soldiers needed to be housed in areas around the barracks. By 2 October there were 2,000 territorials billeted in the city; others were in tents, some remained in their homes. Despite Kate Wester's letter to a local paper praising the conduct of the men she had had billeted on her,[13] the following advert appeared in the *Worcester Daily Times* and indicated the increasing need for accommodation:

RECRUITING

Citizens who are desirous of having
Officers or Men of the Territorial Forces
Billeted in their homes, should apply
Immediately to the

ADJUTANT OR BILLETING OFFICER,

AT THE RESPECTIVE

BATTALION OR BATTERY

HEAD QUARTERS[14]

If some women were coping with looking after men who had volunteered, others were struggling with the difficulties men left behind. Before the end of August 1914 it was noted that

Mr T. H. Griffiths, Hon Secretary of the department caring for the needs of dependents of soldiers and sailors, had now received about 200 applications for relief. Most of the applicants have had the usual Government separation allowance, and it is anticipated that the whole of them by tomorrow will have received it. Temporary relief is being given in many cases, but until there is actual need for the fund to be distributed, the full machinery will not be set in motion.[15]

The following week, it was reported that the dean of the cathedral had brought to the attention of the subcommittee dealing with the relief of dependents of soldiers and sailors in Worcester the case of the wife of a reservist, living in one of the courts in the city, who had been evicted. She was the mother of five children, the youngest of whom was in arrears with her rent.[16] Before the First World War few ordinary soldiers were married, and the wives and widows of those who were relied upon charity for financial assistance. This changed in the first two years of the war, with the introduction of government-funded separation allowances paid to wives. Then, in 1916, the Ministry of Pensions was set up to deal with claims for war disability and war widows' pensions. Such centralised and organised systems provided a safety net and an alternative to charity or the workhouse. These systems, however, took time to establish, and were initially administrated in a clumsy way by charities. For example, the local paper reported that the mother of five had apparently

promised to pay the landlord the arrears as soon as she received her separation allowance. This should have arrived ... but there was some delay. In any case it will arrive in the course of a post or two. When she got back home after a visit to the Guildhall, a notice to quit possession of the tenement had been left for her.[17]

The following week the newspaper carried a suggestion that there were other circumstances which explained the eviction; however, hers was by no means a solitary case, and in January 1915 the *Worcester Herald* suggested soldiers' letters indicated that men's morale was affected by worry over maintenance payments for their wives.[18]

Letters to local papers and reports of meetings indicate that there was a strong awareness of the financial distress that married men volunteering might cause for their families. There was also, among the wealthier groups who administered the charities, a suspicious attitude towards the working classes. Rumours circulated that at least one woman had benefited in the Boer War by requesting assistance from two different charities for two different husbands. Co-ordination, structures and systems were required to prevent over-payment, but a number of women were victims of such systems and there was a chasm that existed between the lives of those administering financial relief and the working women who needed it, something this next letter to the editor of *Worcester Daily Times* in October 1914 tries to address.

Sir – a neighbour of mine whose husband has enlisted, and is away serving his King and country, went today to the Guildhall for the usual five shillings relief, but was told that the issuing of relief had been discontinued. In this case there is a family of four boys and girls all at an age which signifies hearty appetites. This woman's separation allowance amounts to 22s (£1.10p) weekly, which apportioned reasonably works out something like this: Rent 5s (25p), upkeep of clothes at 6d (2½ p) per head per week, 2s 6d (25p) coal (in winter) and absolutely necessary sundries, say another 2s 6d leaving for the whole family of five 12s. This makes no provision for the paying off of debts incurred through the recent bad trade, or for sickness, insurance or anything else. This food allowance works out at about 1d per head per meal. Yet one of the relief officials expressed the opinion that this amount is quite sufficient.

I don't suppose he or any of his family, subsists on 1d per meal, and yet he expects the family of 'Tommy' to whom we are all supposed to be so grateful to do so.

It should be noted also (a fact which had been carefully left unmentioned in the Press) that to make this increased allowance that the Government announced would be given to the soldier's wife, the soldier's pay (if he has three or more children) is being appropriated to the extent of 5s 3d (26p). Thus the bulk of this generous increase is being provided out of the soldier's own pocket.

This woman's husband who is now receiving a paltry 1s and 9d (9p) per week, out of which to find the necessary additions to the Army diet, to find himself and pay for laundry and other expenses.

She therefore out of the money that provides her 1d per meal has to send him something to help out the miserable pittance he has left for his own pocket.

This is not the worst case in Worcester it is typical of many such.

A. Kipling points out: 'It's Tommy this and Tommy that and Tommy go away. But it's "thin red line of heroes" when the guns begin to play.' And this is how Worcester rewards him, while a notice outside the Guildhall announces that the relief fund has reached £3,500.

Is this a sample of the 'Faithful City's' much vaulted patriotism? What is going to be done about it?

Mark Tike[19]

For many housewives, the day-to-day struggle to survive in wartime Worcestershire gravitated around providing their family with a sufficient amount of food. Food hoarding (an option only for the wealthier women whose houses had suitable storage facilities) and shortages meant prices soured and many women struggled to make ends meet. Some of the suggestions to address this were more credible than others, as this letter to the *Worcester Daily Times* indicates:

ECONOMY IN WARTIME
A Simple Plea

The war will soon cause distress to the poor. Let those who can save the peelings of potatoes, carrots, apples etc, and the outside layers of onions, and leaves of cabbage lettuces etc, pea-pods, marrow seeds etc wash them well; let them simmer in water and after straining, add milled breadcrumbs and crusts, milled cheese and some soaked cooked peas or beans or lentils and distribute to the needy or else send to some central place for distribution.

It would mean a little individual trouble but would cost hardly anything and would help a good deal. It is suggested a few leaflets could be scattered, broadcast amongst the poor, advising them to masticate their foods more thoroughly (and thus lessen the bulk needed) and practice gentle but deep and full breathing, and keep the blood clean by sipping hot or cold water first thing in the morning and last thing at night. Our people will need not only all the cheap food but also all the cheap health that can be had.[20]

What the response of the poor working-class housewife might have been to such a letter – should she have bothered to read it – is not recorded. The suggestion that she instruct her family to chew more so they will not need so much food contains a familiar trope which placed increasing pressure on the housewives in the First World War. It lays the responsibility to deal with food shortages or rising prices in her household rather than in the government hands. Eventually this would change, but it would be a slow process.

Initially many of the recipes and much of the advice in newspapers was geared towards those who were comfortably off. It was suggested that, by voluntarily restraining themselves from food hoarding or eating the cheaper foodstuffs, they could ensure the poorer classes had an adequate supply of cheaper foods; bread and potatoes were important staples of working-class diets, but the local newspapers gave recipes for:

PRESSED FOWL – A delicious method of cooking an old fowl and a very appetising dish for hot weather says a writer to an agricultural paper. Have your fowl ready dressed for boiling, place with giblets in a saucepan, partly cover with warm water and simmer gently until bones will slip from meat. Have ready a plain (buttered) mould. Take out the fowl remove skin and bones and press meat into mould; ornament top with hard-boiled eggs and finely chopped parsley. Skim the soup to free it from fat, add ¼ oz gelatin, a tablespoonful of vinegar, a half a teaspoon each of mace, pepper and salt. Strain the soup thus prepared over fowl. Cover down with a plate or saucer to fit mould. Stand till cold and serve with lettuce and tomato salad.[21]

EGGLESS FRUIT CAKE – One breakfast cupful of sugar, three fourths of a cupful of butter, three cupfuls of flour, one half cupful of currants, one half cupful of sultana raison, one cupful of rich sour cream, one-fourth cupful of lemon extract and one teaspoonful of baking soda. Beat the butter and sugar to a cream, add sour cream, flour, soda, flavoring, currants and raisons. Mix and turn into a buttered and floured cake tin and bake in a slow oven for one and a quarter hours.[22]

In 1915 Mrs Florence Petty, known as the Pudding Lady, visited Worcestershire to give a series of talks on cooking to mothers and to social workers.[23] She had been involved with the St Pancras School for Mothers, which aimed to teach working-class housewifery skills, but she had soon decided that attempting to teach in the school on site was next to useless. Instead she visited women in their own homes, giving them lessons and assisting them in learning to cook themselves. Her cookery book, which was already popular when she visited Worcestershire, included recipes for 'Half Pay Pudding' and 'Economical Fritters'. She encouraged substitution of costly products such as eggs with cheaper and home-grown food such as vegetables, and devoted a whole chapter to potatoes. Little wonder that she worked for the Ministry of Agriculture in wartime. Her work was linked to raising the health of families, babies and children. In Worcestershire, babycraft classes were also being organised alongside baby shows[24] to improve the health of the working classes. Recruitment in both the Boer War and the First World War shed light on poor nutrition and health of the poor, with many recruits having to be rejected as unfit. Consequently infant welfare was a focus of much activity throughout the war.

An infant examination and mothercraft competition. From *Berrows Worcestershire Journal*.

The Women's Institute movement, set up under the auspices of the Agricultural Organisation Society to improve the food supply in 1915, echoed some of these concerns. Its slogan, 'For Home and Country', linked the domestic sphere to the national war effort. On 1 March 1916 a public meeting at the Shirehall in Worcestershire was held under the auspices of the County War Agricultural Committee. Among the great and the good of the county who attended, under the chairmanship of Lord Coventry of Croome Park, was Mrs Watt. This Canadian woman was the representative of the Agricultural Organisation Society, with whose support she had founded the Women's Institute movement in Britain. By November 1916 a proposal to start one of the first WIs in the county was passed unanimously in Pershore Masonic Hall. The organisation promoted increased food production and preservation, despite the shortage of sugar – perhaps they were heartened by the Chancellor of the Exchequer's assurance that there would be enough sugar provided for domestic fruit preservation. For many of the women who joined the WI its appeal lay in the companionship, friendship and relief from domestic drudgery that these communal activities offered. Its formation was timely and its demonstrations on wartime food, the use of maize and barley meal and the making of 'really cheap nutritious soup' were probably very welcome.

With the growing intensity of sea warfare and naval blockades, food shortages had by 1916 become more acute and prices were rising fast. The local papers carried reports of discussions in parliament about the doubling of the price of potatoes, which were in short supply. There was anxiety about whether potatoes were being bought up by hotels or exported to allies and the minister responsible addressed the better off in society, appealing to them to voluntarily restrain their food consumption:

To all those who, as many do, consume potatoes twice daily more as a matter of habit than anything else, economise in the use of potatoes and substitute other foods for them, so there may be a better supply for those who are not so well off and for whom a sufficient supply of potatoes at a reasonable price is a very important part of their daily food.[25]

For those in the more rural parts of the county with larger gardens or allotments who could grow their own vegetables, this shortage of potatoes was perhaps not such a crisis, but in Worcester a gift of potatoes from Canada was reported in a local paper.

About 800 sacks of potatoes have been sent to Worcester – part of Canada's gift to the country. Each of the sacks contained 80 or 90 lb of potatoes and these were distributed in the City Police Yard this afternoon to a large number of poor people. The Supply and Demands Sub-Committee of Worcester Relief Committee has charge of the arrangements, Churches and chapels of all denominations in the city sent in the names of people in their various districts and parishes to whom a share of the of the gift would be acceptable, and a list was prepared by the Committee of something like 200 people.

There was a continuous procession of women, armed with bags and baskets and tickets which entitled them to have these filled. Each one received 15 lbs of potatoes and went away with a radiant face and well filled basket.[26]

As the food shortages became more severe and queues grew longer, with reports of a queue of 600 people waiting in

Potato queues in 1916. From *Berrows Worcestershire Journal*.

Worcester for ½ lb of margarine,[27] the efforts to encourage people to voluntarily reduce their food consumption – particularly of fats, meat and bread – increased. The official demonstrator for the Vegetarian Society gave a lecture on vegetarian cookery in Evesham, which was reported to be interesting with much valuable information given, and in the same week a meeting was held in the kitchens of Ombersley Court to provide demonstrations of wartime cookery.[28] In May 1917, The King's Proclamation on the Food Supply was read out in churches, encouraging people to eat less food, although a number of non-conformist clergy in Worcestershire objected to this secular matter being included in a religious service.

Pershore WI set up a communal kitchen in 1917, taking it in turns to be responsible for the catering, but it did not get used as they had hoped and was closed down within a few months. Pig and rabbit clubs were far more successful, as was herb growing, knitting comforts for the troops, toy making and further cookery demonstrations held throughout the region. The food crisis continued to grow worse, however, and the WI Committee in Pershore proposed to scrap having tea and cakes at their meetings due to the food shortage. In 1917 making dog biscuits was banned and there was discussion of doubling the dog tax as non-working dogs began also to be seen as a drain on limited food supplies.

As the war progressed, cajoling and encouragement was supplemented by compulsion and inspection; in Kidderminster the War Savings Committee began to take a more threatening tone towards housewives, warning them of fines for wasting bread. They banned Sunday school outings as they apparently wasted food, and Revd Campbell Lee speaking in Milton Hall explained that the 'battle of the loaf had begun' and warned people against 'calling up the loaf for duty between meals' and requested they resisted having elevenses. Kidderminster was particularly concerned about bread consumption, campaigning through posters, exhibitions and demonstrations, with repeated references to fines for wasting bread in a threatening manner:

KIDDERMINSTER FOOD CAMPAIGN
the Cupboard is the Housewife's Trench
and She Must Defend it
KIDDERMINSTER
FOOD CAMPAIGN

—

BE CAREFUL WITH ALL YOUR FOODSTUFFS
At Bromley a householder was fined £5 for wasting bread
At Bristol two 'bread wasters' were fined £50 and £25 respectively

—

**ALL PATRIOTIC PEOPLE ARE
EATING LESS BREAD**[29]

The rhetoric of threat, the focus on the minutiae of everyday life, a struggle to acquire the necessary food for supper and quandary over whether to have a slice of bread in the middle of the day meant that all housewives' everyday decisions were becoming the subject of governance. In their battles in the shops and with prices they did have some allies, as an increasing regulatory framework governed food prices, supply and consumption. A Mrs Patchett discovered this when trying to deal with a grocer in St Swithins Street who had tried unlawfully to impose conditions on her purchase of sugar. A prosecution led the grocer to be fined £5 after the Chief Constable explained to the court that

Mrs Fanny Patchett went to the shop and bought some groceries. She then went to another counter and asked for a pound of sugar. The assistant a young lady said: 'Anything else, madam?' and she said 'No, thank-you'. The assistant then said 'We have none to spare'. Mrs Patchett said that she knew they had sugar and the assistant replied 'If you buy groceries you can have sugar.' Mrs Patchett said she had just spent 3 shillings at the other counter. The assistant still refused to serve her with sugar and Mrs Patchett said she should report the fact to the Minister of Food'.[30]

In Malvern the War Savings Committee was also keen to promote food economy, although the political tensions and differing attitudes to class and gender are evident in their discussion over their Food Economy Campaign. Dr H. E. Dixoy considered 'that a good deal of waste was still going on, partly because people had not appreciated the urgent need of food economy. He was sure women would be able to give valuable help'.[31] There seemed, however, to be a distinctive shortage of women giving an opinion on or even belonging to this committee, nevertheless Mr W. Evans put an alternative view explaining that he

believed that a great deal of the waste which formerly went on among the poorer classes had been curtailed. If they were going to reduce the bread supply they would starve out the poorer population with whom bread was the staple article of food. He did not want to make a tee-total speech but he thought that the barley at present malted and utilised for this production of intoxicating liquor which were a luxury could be saved and put into the bread.[32]

Although food shortages were experienced by all, their effect on day-to-day housewifery was varied. When it was noted in the Hagley Hall Scrapbook that it was 'very difficult to get food, frequently no butter, margarine and lard. Everyone looks very thin as if a good leg of mutton would do them good, great shortages of cheese and fats of all kinds',[33] different tactics were used to deal with the problem. Money made it possible to substitute a food product in short supply with another one that was not, or which had been stored previously. The issue of queuing was easier to manage if left to servants and if it did not have to be undertaken on top of a week working in a munitions factory. Aware of growing unrest – particularly in urban areas – over food, and anxious that reports of the problems would undermine the morale of troops on the front line in January 1918, food rationing was introduced for what were considered basic foodstuffs: sugar, fats (butter and margarine) butchers' meat, bacon, ham and then jam. Bread was not rationed, but its production was subject to tight controls that governed its size and ingredients to ensure it lasted.

For all women the disruption and difficulty of domestic life in

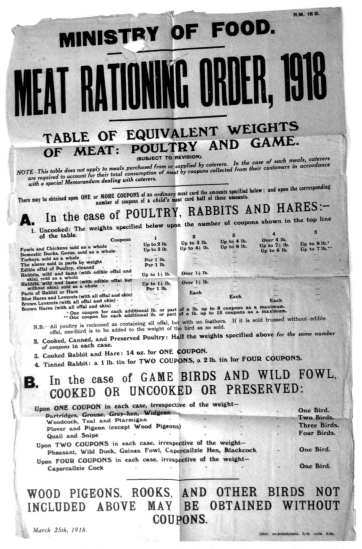

Meat rationing order from 1918. (With thanks to Worcestershire Archive and Archaeology Service)

wartime was compounded by anxiety over their relations at the front. There are few accounts of how women responded when the news they heard was bad, but some survive. Lavinia Talbot, who had grown up at Hagley Hall, kept a diary throughout the war. She had five children; her youngest son Gilbert was nine years younger than any of his siblings. In July 1915 he was on the front line at Ypres while her elder son Ted was home on a visit – her diary entry records,

Very anxious letter from Neville, telling of terrible fighting attack & counter attack at Hooge trench – no news of Gilbert. Almost at the same moment I saw Ted reading something near the door, it made me sure there was bad news. I went up to him and asked what it was. After hesitating he let me see the paper which told of my darling Gilbert being killed … And I knew that most of the light in my life had gone out.[34]

5

Dear Mother, Dear Wife

The bonds between the Worcestershire soldiers and their homes and communities were nurtured by the heavy traffic of letters and parcels that were sent between them and their mothers, wives, friends and family. In 1916, 5 million letters were sent each week from the British Expeditionary Force in France and Belgium to Britain. The post, which could travel from the Western Front to Worcestershire in only two days, was key to the emotional survival of men in the fighting forces, who cherished being able to hold letters written by their loved ones only a few days before. Post from home assured soldiers they were not forgotten, and symbolised the caring and love of the homes they felt they were fighting to protect. Studdert Kennedy, the Church of England vicar from Worcester who ministered to soldiers at the front, described the significance of letters and parcels for the morale of men on the front line. From the third despatch printed 26 February 1916:

When your boy is up the line that letter is needed in another way. He comes back to rest, drenched to the skin and shivering with cold and his first thought is always, so they tell me, letters from home. Picture to yourselves his face as the pile in the Sergeant's hand grows less and less and still his name has not been called. See him turn away and go to his corner without his hope and with the blankness of his heart and remember that next time the letter may be there, the name may be called, and no answer made, because they are carrying something on a stretcher out of the clearing station. The voice that should have answered gladly will never answer anymore.[1]

Men in the armed forces continued to emotionally identify with their families and communities and they wrote particularly to their mothers or wives to ask about their family, friends and pets. In return they received parcels of food, letters and copies of newspapers and magazines. Private Jack Bird, initially of 6th, then the 2nd Battalion Worcestershires,[2] wrote to his mother and father from France in 1916.

I hope you enjoyed your Xmas all right, there was no enjoyment over here for we are miles from anywhere we done no work Xmas day but we were penned up almost nowhere to go. I was glad to get in bed but shan't sleep thinking about home and the children wondering what they had been doing. It is the first year that I have not been able to put anything in their stockings and I hope it will be the last.

And later, on 28 February 1917:

We have been having a rough time of it out nearly all night in no mans land with shells bursting over us it is not a pleasant sensation but you get use to that. I have forgot the taste of beer I have not had any for 6 weeks.[3]

This chapter features the voices of two Worcestershire soldiers and the letters they wrote home. William Brown from Lowermoor, Worcester, joined up in February 1915 and, like many of the young men who were fighting, he was away from home for the first time. His soldier's small book attests that he is five foot, four and three-quarter inches and aged nineteen. He wrote regularly, although often briefly, to his mother, but also to his seven siblings and some friends. His letters sometimes describe his life in training hospital and in the trenches, while others merely express his yearning for any news or communication from home.

Jack, from Tenbury Wells, was married, with a daughter and another child on the way, when he volunteered in 1915. They both served as ordinary soldiers, although Jack's letters indicate he had had more education and was more accustomed to writing; he tried unsuccessfully to get a commission in 1916. Training and injuries meant that both soldiers spent a considerable amount of time – the majority of their war service – well away from the battlefronts. This was a typical experience but was not without its challenges, for many of soldiers had not previously travelled beyond Worcestershire. During these often tedious times, keeping the image and the idea of home alive in the imagination sustained men. Home and family were vital for the emotional survival of men in the armed forces in wartime.

In 1915 Will Brown, who was initially stationed in Devonport, wrote one of his first letters to his mother and sister to let them know how things were going.

Dear Mother and Sister

I had a letter off Frank and he has written the address on for me if you write again. We are expecting to move this week to Tidworth so write before Saturday.

I am getting on quite well but it's a bit rough. We have plenty of food. The time I am writing this is Wednesday February 17th.

I am glad dad is getting better and I hope you are all in good health and happy. The other piece is for Ernie Noake as I want to know how the pigeons is getting on as there is none down here only seagulls and a few german ships whats captured.

With best love to you all

from Bill[4]

His regular letters to his mother during 1915 were mainly about life at home, often asking after the health of his father, who was ill. He was constantly anxious for news of his beloved pigeons, who represented home and freedom for him. The birds were being looked after by his friend Ernie Noake, who is often mentioned in the letters, and sometimes referred to as Ern. However, Will's age was not nineteen, as the entry in his soldier's small book claims, but seventeen. He was one of approximately a quarter of a million lads who signed up underage.

Dear Mother,

I hope you are quite well also dad and grandad. I arrived quite well and safe but I did not write before because I did not know if I was for the front or not you will be pleased to know I is not going because I look too young. I passed the doctor but the Co General told me I have to go through a special course of Swedish guns for about a month. I expect they will send for my birth certificate but send it as they know I am only 17 there is about sixty of us underage and I think they are going to discharge us or we are going all round Worcestershire recruiting but I will write again and let you know. Tell Jack Daniels I will write Friday night when we get paid as this is the last penny I have got. You can keep the slippers or send them which you like but I shall have to buy another pair.

If Ernie Noake enlists write and let me know tell him I am well. Remember me to Amy and Flo. I shall write to them Friday.

With Best wishes

Will

There was, as Will's letter to his mother makes clear, a degree of collusion in the recruiting of boy soldiers by recruitment sergeants, Army personnel and parents. After training in Cornwall, despite his age, Will was sent abroad in October 1915 and wrote home on 1 November 1915.

Dear Mother

Just a few lines hoping to find you and all at home are in good health. I hope Dad does not get any worse. I received your letter quite safe also the paper you sent me which I was very glad to receive. I shall not be able to write every week as you wish me to as I have not enough envelopes and paper to write very often you can send me some and make up a parcel and send me. The post card with the boat on is the one I sailed on it took us twelve days travel that was rather quick as it generally takes more. I should like you to ask Ernie Noake how many pigeons there is and I want you to tell me in your next letter for sure if he enlists I should like him to leave me a couple of pairs of the pied one and a pair of champion you can show him this letter so as he will no what I want. Harry Wedgebury still looks well and he was telling me about Baden enlisting in the land up at Norton I hope he will like it. Tell Aggie that was a nice letter she wrote me and I am glad she goes on with her work alright and I hope she will look after herself now she is going on well. Well I have not said much about sister Flo lately but I hope she will not think me too bad but I hope the two children and herself is going on alright. I think this is all this time

From your Loving Son,

W. Brown

Within a month Will is unwell and removed to Malta; he lets his mother know about it in a letter written on 28 November 1915.

Dear Mother,

Just a few lines hoping to find you in good health also all at home. I am writing to Amy the same time as this. I am in a hospital at Malta with a bad leg it is something the matter with my left knee. I have had it now for about a week and it is very painful. The doctor calls it Synovitis but I hope to be better soon. The last time we were going up to the trenches I got left behind as we had about 3 miles to walk and when I got into the communication trench which is about 2 mile long I had to sit down because I could not hardly walk with all my kit but I happened to be lucky for Harry Wedgebury came along that way and gave me a drop of rum and helped me to get along the best he could. I saw the doctor the next day and he sent me on the boat ready to go to the hospital and I am going on alright now. You won't be able to write until I get back to the trenches but I think you could write as I don't expect to be in here any more than a month or six weeks. Remember me to Flo.

From your loving Son

W. Brown

Stranded in Malta, Will Brown longed for letters and parcels from home, but he was well aware that letter writing took time and money. Nevertheless, some women wrote every week or every day to husbands or sons in different parts of the world, ensuring that they maintained their domestic caring role even though their men were in armed forces. Letters written home from the front were passed around, or sometimes extracts would be copied out and sent on to another relative. This ensured the news was shared around, in a period of time when almost all writing was done laboriously by hand and fewer letters could be written. In 1915 Will wrote to his mother again.

Dear Mother

I have had a letter from Amy. I am glad Jen is busy as I hope she helps you a bit she said she was writing to Frank and told me that he is quite well and that he is at the base having a rest. I am sorry to hear that Charlie Ford is wounded but he is one of the lucky ones as he has been out there since it started. I wrote five letters to different people last week and I have only had one in return. I can't make out Ern Noake as he has not wrote back once yet.

I can excuse you and know you don't have much money but Flo don't write at all I mentioned in my last letter that I was on stretcher bearing. I hope the pigeons are getting on well and don't forget to tell me how the young ones look and how many there is. Ask Ern why he has not wrote. I don't think the letters are getting lost as that is three or four I have wrote and he has not wrote back yet. I think this is all this time.

Closing with best wishes to Dad and Grandad
from your Loving Son

Bill

Write back soon.

Jack's army career began a month after Will's; he left Worcestershire on 9 March 1915 and after getting kitted out in London travelled to Walney House, where he was billeted in North Holmwood,

Dorking, to begin training. He wrote very regular, sometimes daily, letters to his wife. The following is from 17 March 1915.

I am getting on better in my billet now, I have dried up once or twice for Mrs Francis and I get so much in the way of rations that it nearly keeps them as well as us, and so she makes out with a few extras, I do feel fit and what I eat at breakfast would surprise you, I do like the photo of you and Baby. I hope she is not being too spoilt. Are you feeling alright? A few cakes to take out at mid-day would be nice, but you needn't worry, we do very well.

Despite the physical distance between them both, he and his wife struggled to continue their traditional roles; he as the provider and she continuing to take on domestic and caring roles. He was frequently concerned about whether she had enough money, and like many other soldiers he quickly discovered there was a need for him to provide some of his own kit and food.

Both Will and Jack also frequently requested items which were not readily available, such as Woodbines, and in one letter Will requests a handkerchief, saying, 'I want you to try and send me a handkerchief as we cant go out when we like, and I want a handkerchief bad.' One of the responsibilities of women on the home front was to source and supply a range of items, including socks and underwear. Better-off families also sent blankets, helmets, scarves, jerkins, equipment and overcoats to men in the armed forces. Food and tobacco were very common ingredients in parcels, although they did not always travel well; Worcestershire soldiers reported parcels arriving where strawberries had turned into a sludgy mess or rats had nibbled at loaves of bread.

On 23 March 1915 Jack wrote,

I had some quite good news today. I received a voucher from the Worcester Territorial Association for a £10 bounty from the National Reserve, so next pay-day I hope to send you some money. I will keep £2 I want to buy a light pair of boots. I could often wear them in place of my heavy ones and it would be great to rest my feet, I had such a very nice letter from Ted this morning and you are to be <u>sure</u> and tell him if you want anything done. He would sharpen the carving knife for you every day if you got into the habit of putting it out for him when he came in. St Martin's soldiers and Club is simply grand, Billiards, Bagatelle, reading rooms, and a nice canteen where you can get anything you want to eat or drink (bar intoxicants) very moderately. I <u>shall</u> be glad to see you and dear little Babs again. I am so sorry she is worried by those tiresome spots. I am sleeping in a very small bed now, and not having very good nights. For one thing I get drill on my mind and often find myself drilling like mad in the nights. I am always glad of a letter from home, it makes me feel I am not so far away. I haven't seen any primroses growing yet, but have seen some in a little girls buttonhole, I am so well and fit – only one foot at all tender now and I shall have an easy day tomorrow.

Jack and Will's letters indicate they were both concerned their military service would result in their families being short of money. They would both have made significant financial contributions to their households – Jack as the husband and breadwinner, Will as a son living at home. Separation allowance was paid to wives and mothers, but all such systems were new in the First World War and took time to establish.

Four months after he had joined up, Jack's wife gave birth to a baby boy and he wrote on 4 July 1915:

I was wondering how you and the boy are getting on.

He will be a month old on Monday and I suppose you are getting about again. I was glad to hear Nurse had gone. We had another good march on Friday. It was hot and close but might have been worse. It was stupid that we were given such a small ration to march on. We breakfasted at 6 a.m. fell in at 7, marched off and did not get back until 5 – 11 hours on breakfast, banana and 4 Garibaldi biscuits. I have saved a piece of bread and butter from breakfast and had a hard boiled egg in my mess tin, but I was quite hungry when we got dinner at 5:30.

I was so pleased to find two parcels one from Olive and I started on her little cakes at once and gave some away. Ted sent cherries but he had packed them in a composition collar box and most of the cherries were flavoured with camphor. Still they all went the same way, The Reverend Boyd-Carpenter preached us a very good sermon today. I think he is the Bishop of Ripon – such a nice old man.

His next letters were concerned with getting leave to come home and have his son christened. At Christmas 1915 he is still in England, longing to be at home and aware of the family rituals, such as salting the pig, that he is missing.

Dec 19th

I have written for leave for Monday. Of course if I do not get it I shall not be able to come, If I get it I shall be able to start from Ware on 5 a.m. We shall be back in billets in Ware on Tuesday. Mrs G has made me promise if I don't get leave from Christmas to come here. You wouldn't' believe how kind they are. So sorry to think of you salting that pig without me. Do be careful not to slip in the cellar steps. The pig will pay quite well after. I have heard that I am moving billets when I get back to Ware – to a much better one with three nice fellows, Corporals I have wanted to be in with them. They had a young chap with them got drunk and disgraced himself and got chucked out and asked for me. Do put the money your Aunts gave you in the bank for the boy, don't spend it on a jersey. I am supposed to keep you and I want to and so get the jersey and have it entered in account.

Neither the billet nor Christmas leave turned out as Jack had hoped, and he spent Christmas at the vicarage.

Dec 28th

There is a chance I may come this weekend. It'll only be a few hours mind but I should like to see you and the kiddies. I went over to Stansted again yesterday to help with a Parish Tea. It was done so nicely but not as many turned up as they had expected. It was such a rough dark night. Mrs G asked me to come as often as I could especially next Sunday but I am hoping to be in Tenbury. I walked over to Hertford on Sunday morning to see the damage that the Zeppelins did. A good deal of it has been repaired, but still a lot to be seen. I expect you had dinner and tea at Ashfield didn't you? Were the kiddies good? Poor old Frank to be rushed off on Christmas Eve. I ought to think myself lucky to have been in England so long.

Meanwhile Will Brown remained in Malta for all of December 1915, spending his first Christmas away from his family. Like many soldiers he was often short of the paper needed for letter writing. Canteens set up by charities such as the Young Men's Christian Association (YMCA) in rest, recuperation and recovery areas and at transit points offered letter writing materials and comforts of various types to soldiers. Will makes use of these materials in Malta to write a series of quick notes on YMCA-headed notepaper during January 1916.

Dear Mother,

   I received your letter 4th Jan. I don't want you to write to the war office as I am quite safe out here. I want you to give that postcard that I sent the letter to Ern Noake and write back and tell me if Becky has brought the trap down. If Ern enlists I expect you will be able to manage those six pigeons for me. I have not received any books or papers you said you have sent. Closing with best wishes to Flo and all at home,

From Bill

On 13 January 1916, he wrote, 'I am expecting to go away, back to Salonika, so write back soon,' but instead he remains in Malta and at the end of January he again writes to his mother, concerned about his pigeons.

Dear Mother

   I am writing hoping to find you in good health also all at home as I am in the best of health. I don't want you to let the pigeons sit their first lots of eggs so you must take them away from them, I am expecting to go back to Egypt soon but will write as soon as I get to know. I excuse the writing I will write more next time from your ever Loving Son

Bill

He is pleased when early in February he hears he is finally leaving Malta to join his battalion again and writes to let his mother know when he has arrived safely in Egypt on 23 February 1916. His letters continue to be preoccupied with home, reassuring his mother that he is going on well, requesting letters, cigarettes and writing materials and giving instructions for the care of his pigeons. On 12 March 1916 Will wrote,

Dear Mother

I am writing to you hoping to find you and all at home in good health as I am quite well at present. I received five letters here three from you one from Angie and Baden, I have wrote to Mr Noke tell Ern, also tell him I will write to him again as soon as possible. I hope you have done what I asked you to as I expect there will be some more young birds soon, Remember me to Mrs Wedbury also Flo. Frank has not written to me yet. Blessing with best wishes
From your loving Son

By the end of March he has been transferred to the Western Front but finds time to write.

Mother

Amy sent me a cake and a few cherries which I was very glad to receive from her. Don't forget to tell me how Dad and Grandad are getting on and the children. I might have my photo took soon but I don't know when because I only get three shillings a week now so I shall have to put a bit up for a week or two. I wrote a letter to Ern and Jack last week but they have not wrote back yet. I wrote and told Harry Allen to come for those pair of young ones [pigeons] so don't forget to tell me if he has fetched them he has not wrote back yet I don't know why without the letter has got lost. I am glad to hear Franks alright ask Flo if she knows Ern Smith that used to live by us in Blackfriars he is at the front but he has got interie fever. I hope you are feeding the pigeons well I will try and send a shilling every fortnight if you like just to help you a bit. Amy wrote and told me that Ben had a regular job along with a gardener she said she helps you a bit. Don't forget to ask Ern and Jack if they have received my letter I wrote Jack's Thursday and Ern's on Friday. I think this is all this time with best of love

From Bill

Will Brown's letters emphasise the importance of any contact with home. While we know his letters assured his mother he was still safe, we have no record of his mother's response to his letters or her experience of war as she waited for news. Will's letter from France just after Easter 1916 seems to emphasise the emotional significance of his mother and home; he repeats the word 'mother' several times in the letter.

Dear Mother

I am writing hoping to find all at home also yourself in good health. I am quite well at present.

Well mother I received your letter you posted on Easter Monday also the paper.

Dear mother I should like you to send me a pigeon book you can get one from knots down by the Bridge.

I am writing to Amy at the same time as this and I hope I shall soon have an answer as I have only had one this last fortnight.

Dear mother I want you to keep that meaty young one in case one of the old ones go bad. [He is referring to his pigeons] If Ern gets called up I hope you will keep them for me just the same.

Well mother I hope you had a good time Easter but I expect it would have been better if I had been home. Remember me to Mrs Wedgbury tell her I have not seen Harry.

Closing with best
Wishes to all
From your
Ever Loving
Son
Will.

On 10 July 1916 Will Brown, aged eighteen and a half years, was killed in action in France. The following year his father also died from a lung condition he had contracted when working down the mines.

Will died just ten days after the Battle of the Somme had begun and, given the hopes pinned on this battle to break the stalemate on the Western Front, it is not surprising that Jack was also sent to France in June 1916. Jack, however, was back in Britain before the battle had commenced, already injured, as he explained on Tuesday 27 June:

Well we had about a 10 mile march last night – got into billets soon after 11. We were all fairly wet though – settled down to sleep soon after 12. About an hour and half after that they began shelling us and I was fortunate enough to get a wound in my left arm. I may be in England the day after tomorrow! I think it is ridiculous sending me back but I am told it will take a long time to heal. I believe I am the only casualty. I am now out of the danger zone as in the Casualty Clearing Station – going back to base tomorrow.

Jack's convalescence took place in a hospital in Scotland, after which he was posted down to the South near Winchester, from where he wrote to his wife on 22 November 1916:

Thank you so much for the parcel of cake and apples. The cake will be so useful. The meals we get here I consider are shocking. I have been spending a lot on cakes at the YMCA or I should be famished. They must be making a lot out of the Catering Allowance made by the Gvt. per head. I saw the Board of Officers the other day, but still haven't seen the Colonel and time keeps going on.

Once again Jack and his wife were apart at Christmas in 1916 and in his letter on 18 December Jack admitted there was no chance of leave and suggested to his wife, 'You had better make arrangement to go somewhere, I should think Ombersley would be most convenient.' He wrote on 27 December to say that he was to be transferred to the School of Farriers and told how he had boiled and divided up the Christmas pudding she sent him, explaining that he divided it into ten pieces to share with his companions and remarked that 'it was very good'.

Jack remained in England during 1917; his letters suggest the growing stresses of army life as he undertook training courses, juggled his limited finances and remained concerned about his family. On 20 October he wrote to his wife.

Thank-you very much for your letter, I know you have your time well occupied but I do miss your letters when they don't come. This week I feel I have been giving you a dose of your own medicine for I have simply been writing notes as hard as I could go, every minute of spare time, I am not a quick writer and sometimes have a job to get them down roughly because the lecturers has given them our so fast. I had to stay in Camp this evening and was polishing up all afternoon but really I ought not to have been put on it. Every evening I have been writing to 9.30 earliest, but thank goodness I am as near as no matter up to date.

It is very nice to think of Boy quite well again. I hope he will keep so, I was very glad Dick and Mary managed to get home for the weekend. I wish you could have gone too. Don't worry too much about saving. I am quite sure you are not the least extravagant. There are a great many people not saving at all judging by the parcels some fellows receive. I have given up trying to save 5/- a week, There is 6d for washing and if I come here and have 2 teas at 1/- each that is half the weeks money gone in two days. At the end of the month the washing fund is refunded. There is 4d or 6d for a concert and if we have a bad breakfast I run and get a cup of tea and a slice of cake – 2½d, and there's not much left. I had arranged to go to Winchester to an organ recital in the Cathedral with Henderson but of course I couldn't go.

In 1918 Jack was sent to France, writing from Folkestone before embarkation on 28 April.

So far so good. Quite a good time a little rain when we got in about 5 a.m. We all hope we shall go back to 1st Barr. We are not allowed out of camp. The place has been altered around here out of all recognition, I think of the good times we had.

On reaching the base camp at Étaples, Jack found things were chaotic and was upset to discover he was to be attached to the London Fusiliers, whom he describes critically as a 'Bright Badge and Button' regiment. He writes from the School of Musketry on 9 May 1918.

I finished up my last letter rather suddenly to catch the post. This is Thurs, so you may get it on Monday. It is the most beautiful evening, you would enjoy the view which I now have. The camp lies in a valley the Musketry school on the side. The ground rises very steeply and I am sitting on top and have a grand view. Below me to the left it the village church and beyond that a much larger church and village. It is so clear the aeroplanes are so high you can hardly distinguish them from birds except for the humming. I have met 2 or 3 of our men – one in at the Lewis gun school next door – the others are up the line. I have been for walks with the one at the School the last day or two and it makes life much pleasanter. The weather has been very hot yesterday and today and my face has got burnt and is a bit sore. I am longing for a letter and think it takes from 4 to 6 days so I shall begin to look out next Mon or Tues; I expect the garden is looking nice but hope Father has got a gardener. Did the beans come up alright?

Jack was moved into the trenches on 22 May but his letters remained focussed on his Worcestershire community and the minutiae of everyday domestic life for both himself and his wife. He downplays the danger he is in, perhaps because he does not want to worry his wife. He wrote on 29 May:

Thank-you for the letter dated 22nd. Now there is only one unaccounted for. By the same post I received the Tenbury Ad. and Parish Mag. and thank-you for both. I like the snaps very much indeed, both children look fine and jolly. The boy in particular looks older and bigger, I think a proper little boy. If I am in time don't bother about the soap box, the chap sleeping next to mine had it all the time. He is perfectly honest but untidy and careless, I asked him to look through his things which he did in a sort of way, but after having two soap boxes for about a fortnight he at last awoke to the fact that one must be mine. I have written only a short note to Henderson besides the letters I have written to you and must buck up and write some but we may be going out for a rest or something like rest shortly, and I shall have more opportunity?

How is the school kitchen going? Do you get as many children as at first? I am glad to think you have had Mary for a week, and now I hope you have Miss Amphlett for a bit. I am not going to worry about Father, he seems to have good appetite and goes about. I should think it's only the heat you seem to have had of late that has pulled him down. 'Jerry' thinks we want livening up a bit now, or else he wants to get his own back. He is pretty harmless. They are just coming round for letters. They had to go up so far to be censored and probably get to the base by Friday and then on.

Again his stay in the trenches was short, he got trench fever and in a letter sent in mid-June reported that the 'M.O. ordered me to Hospital and I got as far as the 1st Field Dressing Station – stayed one night and on to the C.C.S. yesterday. The Batt[alion] I hear moved off yesterday. I have a slight temp and pains.' His recovery in hospital was slow and it was not until 18 September that he was able to write.

It is nice to have something a little interesting to write about. Today I can tell you that I have been transferred back to the 2/15 Batt. At present I have only got the badges no black buttons and no 15th No. so I retain my Fusilier No. and cannot leave the base until my No. comes up so I may be here for another 2 or 3 days. Did I send my wooden framed mirror home? I do so I wish I could get another piece of glass put in, I cannot get anything so useful and strong. I bought one for 2/6 before I left Blighty and it broke in no time. I am using a piece of broken glass or borrowing. I hope the next letter will be in a green envelope. I heard from a 15th man that Henderson was expecting to come on draft but he has not turned up here. He may have gone to another base. I should like to have seen him. Do you think you could get ½ doz (postcards) of you and the children, the same proof you sent me – shall you want it back? They must be that particular one.

He sent a quick postcard on 27 September.

I left the base Tues morning and am now at Batt. Base I expect to go up to the Batt, this evening Friday. Will write you a decent letter as soon as possible but thought you would like a card in the meantime We arrived here yesterday dinnertime – some journey. Will write tomorrow or next day certain.

Jack was killed in action on 28 September 1918 at about 7 p.m.

6

Voices of Some Very Different Experiences of War

Perhaps it is because of *Blackadder* (BBC 1989) that many people assume that all young men spent the war in the trenches, but this was by no means the case. As the last chapter demonstrated, even those who were foot soldiers spent relatively little time in the trenches; estimates are about five or six days in a month. There were, however, a number of other experiences for Worcestershire's youth, some of whom served in the Royal Flying Corps or the Navy, while others spent months or years as prisoners of war. There were also those who were morally opposed to participation in war and who became conscientious objectors.

The conflict at sea was increasingly important as the war progressed; both Britain and Germany attempted to operate naval blockades to prevent the import of food and other necessary supplies. German submarines (U-boats), particularly after the sinking of the *Lusitania* in 1915, were seen as a particular threat; ships from then on tended to travel in convoys. Furthermore, the British forces fighting in Europe needed supplies constantly shipped across the Channel to them; the wounded also had to be brought back to Britain and reinforcements sent to France. One Worcestershire youngster described to his brother in a letter his experience in the Navy in 1918:

Having been at sea for three weeks I have no opportunity to reply to your letter … We have been continuously running between Devenport and Folkestone and Portsmouth to Le Havre and Cherbourg. On March 9th whilst bound for Le Havre a large transport belonging to the convoy was torpedoed a short distance off our starboard beam.

We sent a wireless message to Portsmouth for two tugs to come to her assistance which arrived three hours later. She did not sink though she was very low in the water … She is now in dry dock with others being repaired.

So thick was the fog the next few days that we were compelled to tie up alongside one another in mid channel for two and half days. We were short of provisions at the outset and were returning to get a fresh supply, those 2½ days we fed in an odd pattern on Navy biscuits, bully beef and water. The sights that you see in the Navy are indeed worth seeing. I like to see the lighthouses flashing and the seaport towns …

About eight days ago at dawn we sighted a German submarine … resting on the stations. The other watch and stokes sleeping below rushed on deck in their draws and bare feet some falling over one another in their eagerness to bag the sub before she dipped. I smiled grimly and waiting for a signal my heart was rushing round like the revolution's of an electric fan. Then two successive terrific crashes rang out. I thought we were torpedoed but soon found out we had released depth charges weighing approximately 300 lbs each. Panes and electric glasses were shattered from the shock of the explosion and put the finishing touches on waking the men who had been sleeping below who were rubbing their eyes and asking what's up. We have reason to believe we sank her though there were no signs of her destruction such as of oil or floating debris.

You do not think the sea would suit you doubtless you will be convinced it would not when you have read my brief description of how rough it can be at times. A little while back off Cherbourg the sea was so rough that our vessel seemed as though she were looping the loop. For over two hours I never knew whether I was standing on my hands or feet I was so sick.[1]

He had probably never been aboard a ship before joining the Navy and similarly those from the Worcester regiments who were attached previous to the Royal Flying Corps were unlikely to have any experience of flying. Their training was rudimentary and they often went into active service with only fifteen hours of solo flying; the planes themselves were not particularly robust and the attrition rate was high. Sir Hugh Chance, after being educated at Eton, joined the Worcestershire Regiment in 1915 and was attached to the Royal Flying Corps in April 1915; after training at a brief posting in Castle Bromwich and Dover he was posted to France in August 1916 and stationed in Fienvillers, from where he flew the raid described below:

After lunch on September 15th, we were sent out (27 Squadron) in pairs to bomb trains. A Canadian, by name P. C. Sherren (he was later killed in an air crash after the war), and I set off together, crossed the lines at a good height and came down low to look for trains. We spied one steaming along on a single line near Gouzeaucourt and I flew along behind it at about 500 feet, 'pulled the plug', and let go my two 112lb. bombs. The first fell at the side of the train, but the second seemed to make a direct hit on the engine, which stopped, emitting clouds of smoke and steam. Sherren dropped his two bombs on the rear coaches and round we flew to examine the damage. I was flying one of the newly delivered planes with a 160 horse-power engine and circling over the village of Gouzeaucourt I realised that I was being machine-gunned from the ground and that bullets were hitting the plane. So I quickly opened the throttle and as I passed over the village let fly with my Lewis gun which was carried pointing down to earth. I saw a German soldier walking with a girl in the street, but I don't suppose my bullets disturbed them. Determined not to run any further risks, I climbed steadily until I reached an altitude of 15,000 feet which was pretty well the Martinsyde's ceiling. On landing at Fienvillers I thought I bumped more than usual and on taxi-ing to a halt found that both tyres had been punctured by bullets and one of the longerons behind my seat had been severed. I reported to the Squadron Commander, Major 'Crasher' Smith. So I was lucky to get away unscathed as there were several bullet holes in the wings. As I was flying over the battlefield I noticed two black objects in one of the ruined villages where fighting was taking place – I think it was Flers.[2]

His luck did not continue to hold; on a bombing raid on 17 December his plane was hit. He crash landed in occupied France, set fire to his plane so that it would not fall into enemy hands and for the rest of the war was a prisoner of war. He was held first at Osnabrück and then from 1917 till the end of the war at Clausthal. As an officer he was not expected to work and conditions were not entirely unpleasant. He began to keep a diary of his life in the camps on 15 October 1916.

Meat for lunch. Lovely day with blue sky and white clouds but heavy shower when at lunch. In the afternoon we were ordered into the canteen by the Commandant who told us what rooms we were to occupy upstairs on the first floor. We were also told we were going to have two hot baths weekly, a reading room, walks, use of the riding school for badminton and that a bookseller would come up from town once a week. Moved into new room – Zimmer 68 – about 5 p.m. Molloy (Dorset Regt. and R.F.C.), Money (East Yorks Regt. and R.F.C.), Helder (Royal Fusiliers and R.F.C.), Saunders (Middlesex Regt. and R.F.C.) and myself. The room is exactly the same size as our old one but on the first floor. Quite a view from the window and much brighter. A cupboard with drawers to hold food. We hear this evening that the Russians have started a new offensive, also that heavy fighting was taking place at Sailly Sallisel (Somme) on 12th inst. Played bridge after appel – Molloy and self versus 'Von' and 'Wingers'. (Saunders was nicknamed 'Von' after the German General in Turkey.)[3]

Arthur Chaytor Pepper was commissioned in to the Worcestershire Regiment in February 1915, and went out to Egypt in December that year. He was seconded to the Royal Flying Corps the following year and learnt to fly, gaining his pilot's wings in December 1916. He was then posted back to France where, on 6 April 1916, he was shot down on a photographic reconnaissance mission over enemy lines in France. The letter to his mother, whose health was far from good, informed her:

A. C. Pepper learning to fly in Egypt.

Your son went down on a photographic Reconnaissance with 5 other machines. The formation of the machines was attacked by German machines. 3 out of our 6 did not return. One was observed to go down in flames and the other … it is not certain about. Of course there is a great deal of hope that your son managed to land on the German side of the lines without further mishap. It is believed that machine which went down in flames was a Mr Bayley's from what the other people tell me. I do not know how long it takes for the Germans to let people know the names of their prisoners. At any rate it would be within 2 months of the day they were missing. I really think there is a good chance of your son being all right. Please accept my sincerest sympathy.[4]

After what must have been an interminable wait, his family heard via the Central Prisoners of War Committee on 18 May 1917 that he was a POW. The experiences that he had endured during that period of time would have been impossible for them to imagine; he recorded them in a diary, beginning with how he had left the aerodrome at 9.30 in bad weather.

My machine too fast so had to zig zag. Hit by 'archie' under left wing. Then attacked by three albatross scouts. Observer Lt W L Day

A. C. Pepper in uniform, and soon after his capture in a POW camp.

Border Regiment shot almost immediately. Control lever jammed. Shot by bullet through right arm. Three shots through dashboard and 7 or 8 through engine cowling. Machine riddled and engine stopped with cloud of smoke. Came down from 8500 feet with only tail gadget working. Hit ground and turned over. Cut face. Taken by infantry to ****** a major who gave me rotten coffee. Doctor dressed my arm. Was then taken to a cellar and examined by German Flying Corps Officer who then took me by car to Douai Barracks. Arm dressed again. 4 o'clock had BB and T in guard room. Was then taken to room 26 a cell with a jailor walking up and down jangling keys.

The following day he did little; the food was pretty awful and he noted that he was 'horribly depressed', and as a young man of not yet twenty-one he wrote home to his mother. His next letter home begins to give an inkling of the anguish, fear and depression that this very young lad experienced as a prisoner of war in a foreign country, injured and depressed and remembering his friend Doug, who he had seen die.

My own darling, darling Mums.

How I wish I could send you a cable or wire telling you that I am safe. I think my heart will break worrying about your anxiety. But as soon as you receive these letters there will be no need to worry any more as I am as safe as houses. Oh how I love you Mums, darling. God in his goodness will help keep you safe and sound for … I know. We will pray to Him that this war will be over very soon so that I can return to you all. Am in a cell in some old … barracks here. You can hear the jailer walking up and down the passage with his bunch of keys. I expect they will send me to somewhere in Germany. After the last few days the sooner the better. I am living in a state of continuous nightmare and can hear poor old Doug shouting 'Pepper I'm hit' as though he were in the room. God bless you darling till the end of the war.

Cannot write anymore. Kiss everyone for me. Give Dad my love

Yr devoted

Chaytor

A couple of days later, on what was Easter Monday, still depressed, he knocked on the wall to disturb the rats and recorded that there was an

answering tap from next room. Got poker to work. Discovered Adams from Edgbaston also depressed. Had great conversation and felt better for it.

By the next day, after an interview with an intelligence officer, he was pleased to note in his diary:

Moved with Adams to room with four other chaps. Robinson V. C. Bulter … and Warburton. Felt actually happy at last. Adams and self slept in different rooms. Bribed a corporal to get us grub etc. Bombardment of ***** very distant. Air raids of ours every night on Douai Aerodrome. Woke me up every night.

Two days later on 12 April he wrote that

in afternoon given a bath. Clothes fumigated. French peasants all bowed. Took leather coat and thigh boots. Given civilian cap, coat and boots and *puttees*. Went Douai station 9.00 – enatrainyed 11.30 in wee 3rd class carriage. Night on train absolutely no sleep. Arm bad.

The arrangements over the next few days were haphazard as he travelled by train, slept on benches or stayed in hotels. He was taken to Mons and then entrained again for Karlsruhe. On 17 April he reached the camp and recorded in his diary:

Clothes fumigated again and had hot bath. Meanwhile room and clothes searched. 6 of us moved to camp 5.30. fags F pen taken away. All money changed into special p of w money. Very sorry to part with Dads present. Put in hut with chap called ***.and Butler. Fairly comfortable but absolutely nothing to do. Bought lot of things from canteen. V. ex. & little use.

The next letter home may have done a little to ease his mother's anxiety, but only a little:

Mums Darling

Do hope you have received my post card with address which I sent yesterday. I have not written before then for a few days for reasons which I will not give. The last few (2) days in France saw the end of our own close confinement. They put six of us into one room all day & 2 of us slept out in another room at night. Robinson V.C. was one of the party and it was <u>very</u> much better. We used to try & play auction with homemade cards & we had to teach Robinson & another chap how to play.

It was wonderful how it passed the time in that crowded little room. On the morning of the 12 they took us all out to be fumigated & disinfected in the evening we started off for the station. [CENSORED] Will not say anything about the railway journey except that it seemed never ending. We are now in a building about ½ mile away I believe from the camp. It is of course nice being together but it is fearfully difficult trying to pass the time.

What kind of grub we shall get in camp? Have a good idea. Anyway tea tablets/Burroughs & Well leaves only, Milkmaid cocoa au lait, tinned butter, occasional tins of chocolate biscuits. Swiss milk (condensed), Plain chocolate etc. But I expect you will know. It is pretty certain that something supplementary will be very nice in fact my mouth is watering already. Oh by the way soap is essential also buttons. As regards paying for these things I think we still have our pay in Cox's and I will send cheques occasionally. Will you ask anyway. Talk about mouths watering – you have only just to mention beef or butter or something to have ours streaming. How is everyone at home? I <u>do</u> hope well & that you have heard where I am now. We are given £3 per month here I believe but can get more otherwise.

Yesterday I gave them a cheque for £10 on Cox's cheque which was being cashed thro' the **** embassy. I expect the rate of exchange will be hefty tho'. Now darling as regards parcels I don't know.

Dad if it is possible for me to give power of attorney from here and if so if it can be arranged. My will by the way is sent to Cox's so will you write them about it. My *** that was lost in France is gone for good I am afraid. You might ask Cox's if it is possible to claim for it will you, if so I can give you a full list of the contents it ought to be about £20 – £30. Am enclosing a cheque now which has just been given me for £10. If Cox's are still collecting my pay it will go through alright.

I am afraid my letters in the beginning were pretty rotten and depressing but I could not write any brighter. I am awfully sorry for it now but do you know how I broke down completely when I started to write & it took me about 3 hours at intervals to write them. I shall have a lot to tell you when I return. It is practically impossible to say much in a letter. Well darling will say adieu now. Am enclosing a letter to the A.C. will you post it to him. My address you know. Dearest darling.

All my love to everyone. I do hope you are keeping fit.

Yrs & lots of love

Yr devoted

Chaytor

His diary over the next few weeks records his daily life: experimenting with frying potatoes in sardine oil, getting parcels and letters, and his health problems. He had been injured in the arm when he was shot down, and a bout of tonsillitis and a 'pretty hefty temperature' had put him in hospital again where he recorded 'cannot eat or drink anything except a pretty awful tea substitute'. On 22 April he noted,

Again not a wink of sleep, am feeling very down. He is giving me a dose of morphine tonight so hope for a better night. About a 100 chaps went off today for Heidleberg. … The … Corp in charge of hosp. is a <u>topping</u> chap everyone in love with him.

His diary also talks of the kindness of some of those who worked in hospital – one brought him soup made by his wife – but with

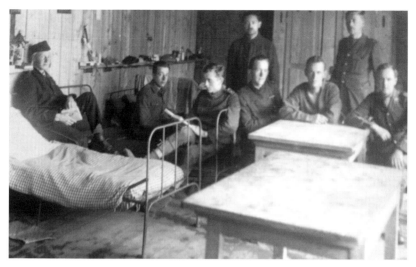

A. C. Pepper in hospital in a German POW camp.

no appetite, his 'head splitting' and having to sleep on a most uncomfortable straw mattress, he was not in good spirits. A few days later, still feeling as 'weak as a kitten' and having lost a lot of weight, he got up at last. On 2 May he recorded, 'Had a supper of sausage and cocoa supplied by Paddy. Had one or two strolls but very tiring. Sausages for supper.' It was nearly two more weeks before he was discharged from hospital and begun to get used to the routines of prison life, noting on 10 May,

Had photo taken. The Corp brought me some goods very exp. but good. Wrote P C and cheque for Mess. Had a bath and washed shirt. Had a long confab. Lights out 9oc in future. Punishment for men who started tunnelling. Went walk with Robinson.

Over the next couple of months his life began to settle into the prison routines. He sent home copies of the camp newspaper indicating the range of activities they could engage in, noting that he had wine on his twenty-first birthday, what he read, ate and how he passed the time; for obvious reasons, there is no mention in his diaries of the tunnelling activities that prisoners engaged in.

Inside a German POW camp room.

He remained in the camp until December 1918, when he returned home in time for Christmas.

A. C. Pepper's memorabilia contains numerous images of plays and concerts the prisoners put on and in this he was not unusual. The Dudley-born actor and film director James Whale developed his dramatic skills when he was an inmate in Holzminden POW camp in Lower Saxony, Germany. He was one of six children of a Black Country blast furnace man, and having joined the Worcestershire Regiment in 1916 he became a second lieutenant. He was captured leading a raid on a fortified Flanders farm in 1917, and spent the rest of the war as a POW participating in numerous prison productions. War was a theme in many of the films that he was later to work on.[5] These POWs were, however, officers; ordinary soldiers were treated differently and usually expected to work. Private Joseph Webb of the 3rd Worcesters was wounded and taken prisoner at Ypres, on 25 October 1914. When interviewed at the end of the war he praised the care he had received in the field hospital but had found the journey from the front to the German POW camp difficult:

Drama and concerts were a popular pastime in POW camps.

Journey to Minden – After that I was taken to Minden, but the journey which took three days and two nights was very bad and my wounds were not dressed. On the way some people came round with food, but when they saw we were English they slammed the door on us. There were about 50 of us in the Truck and nobody to do anything for us.

Once at Minden he was put in hospital and well cared for,

although he felt food was insufficient. When questioned about his treatment in 1918 he was relatively positive:

Difference in Treatment – I think the Germans treat the French better than they do the English, but they don't like the Russians, who have to eat what other people cannot, and the Russians are made to do more work than the English. The English are being treated, I think, better now. At first they used to call us swine, but now a man is put in prison for that. The Germans used to tell is that we ought not to have come into this war as we were only fighting for money. I believe the reason why they treat us better now is because they have heard that their own prisoners in England are being well treated – they owe that.

Parcels – I was able to write and received my first letter at Minden, and after that parcels and letters arrived pretty regularly. The food reached me all right though the bread was not always in good condition – it seemed better when packed up in boxes.

Camp – I have been in, I think, one of the biggest camps in Germany. I should say there were about 16,000 there, out of which 200 would be English.

Cruelty – I heard stories of ill-treatment, but I never actually saw any cases of cruelty.

Work – they made us work – not too hard – about one week on eight weeks. The prisoners worked in mines or in the salt works but I never heard of any being engaged on munitions.[6]

The POWs were something of a *cause célèbre* in Worcestershire; numerous charities and events raised funds to send them parcels, cards and comforts. In Britain there were, however, others who were imprisoned because of their refusal to fight: the conscientious objectors. The introduction of full military conscription in Britain through the Military Service Act of January 1916 was contentious,

A Worcester farmers' sale for the POW fund in 1918.

with members of the cabinet resigning in protest; one of the compromises reached introduced the concept of conscientious objection. Under the terms of the Act, applications for exemption from military service were heard by local military tribunals organised at municipal and district council level. Recourse was then available to a county appeal tribunal; in Worcestershire this was inevitably chaired by J. W. Willis Bund.[7] There were four grounds for exemption: undertaking work of national interest, provision of subsistence to a dependent, infirmity and ill-health, and conscientious objection; nationally around 16,500 men formally raised an objection to undertaking military service on the grounds of conscience and around 1,500 'absolutists' refused to co-operate with the war effort in any way.

The makeup of the tribunals was such that an important place was given to a military representative, so this did not necessarily create the basis for even-handed judgements. Though press reports suggest they often did represent the feelings of the general public in their incomprehension and disgust at the objectors who came before them, this was not always the case. They were not helped in their deliberations by national confusion as to the basis on which conscientious objection could be raised and the level of exemption from service that could be awarded to COs, as they

119

became known. It was only through emerging case law, further clarification from central government in the summer of 1916 and the constant work of groups in support of conscientious objection that even a semblance of consistency and humanity was established. Local tribunals were highly resistant to granting total exemption for COs, and even when granting conditional exemptions seemed to have insisted that COs should experience a degree of personal sacrifice in return, for example giving up urban employment to work on the land, or white-collar work to go into a factory. They seemed not to recognise or realise that the objection, in many cases, was not just to killing but to accepting any military discipline or work that might be deemed to support the war effort. As it was, COs at best faced public humiliation and, at worst, repeated appearances in court, imprisonment and the full force of military discipline. Conscientious objection was no coward's way out, as some at the time chose to portray it.

The unsympathetic attitude of the county council – and by extension the appeal tribunal which shared the same chairman and a number of members – is indicated by a news report from spring 1916 of a discussion by the council entitled

Worcester Grammar School Master's Conscientious Objection
Vigorous Protest at County Council

...

Mr. T. W. Parkes said ... A conscientious objector to military service was an abomination, and a man who at this time was ashamed or afraid to serve his King and country had no right to teach boys ... Mr. Hobson hoped Mr. Parkes would not press this ... He had made a public protest, and most of them sympathised with what he had said, but, rightly or wrongly, the Act of Parliament had given the master the right to do what he had done. Probably now that the matter had been mentioned, the Governors would deal with it.[8]

A resolution on 5 June 1916 noted that despite labour shortages, 'this County Council do[es] not employ men having a conscientious objection to Military Service'.[9] In Worcestershire, objectors were relatively rare and seem to have been largely regarded with fascination rather than as a serious threat to the war effort. Records of tribunal meetings were regularly published in the local press and these provided great detail of special-interest cases such as those of conscientious objectors. It is very unusual that the record books of the Redditch military tribunal have survived (most such records were systematically destroyed soon after the war ended), and this provides an indication of the scale of the task facing the tribunals, with its 3,446 entries.

The local tribunals and county appeal tribunals found themselves inundated with claims for exemption in early 1916. Nationally the vast majority of the nearly 2 million cases heard by tribunals were not about conscience at all; however, it became clear to many, even those who did not agree with the COs, that tribunal decisions on matters of conscience were not just or consistent. An article in the *Worcestershire Echo* on 14 April 1916 observed,

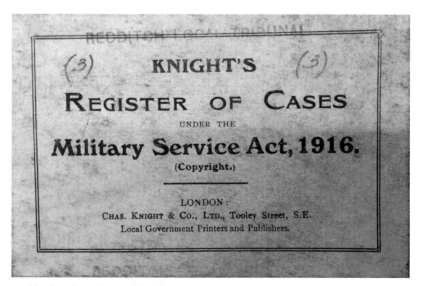

Redditch tribunal record book.

The position of the conscientious objector in strict law appears to be undefined and, in the absence of an authoritative decision, the tribunals are deciding according to their several predilections, with complete honesty no doubt, but without uniformity. According to some lawyers, exemption from full service can be given upon only one of two alternatives – non-combatant service on the one hand and an agreement to do 'work of national importance' on the other. This view is contested by those who hold that an absolute exemption may be given, and nothing less will satisfy those who protest that they will take part in no work which will increase the efficiency of the nation for participation in the war.[10]

The Dean of Worcester, W. Moore Ede, was one of those who spoke out nationally; his dialogue in the weekly dispatch was reported in the *Worcestershire Echo*:

Mr. Asquith, on whose word we are all accustomed to rely, promised that conscientious objectors should be exempt from military service. This exemption was embodied in the Act, and faith should be kept with the conscientious objector.

The tribunals are, of course, bound to see that the plea is not put forth as an excuse for shirking military service; but when members of tribunals, sometimes men notoriously irreligious, attempt to argue as to the teaching of the New Testament, there is something worse than a travesty of justice.

The arbitrary actions of the tribunals are arousing bitter ill-will, which may be suppressed during the war, but is creating a temper fatal to the acceptance after the war of the mildest form of national service if there be any element of compulsion in it.[11]

This prescient piece appeared in the *Daily News*, 2 September 1916:

Sir – some time ago I was brought into contact with some conscientious objectors who were awaiting court martial at our local barracks for refusing military service. With the approval of the commanding officer I had some interviews with them, and endeavoured to show them what I regarded as the fallacy of their objections.

As they remained unconvinced, I advised them to treat the authorities with civility and accept quietly whatever punishment was awarded. They were sentenced to 118 days' hard labour, and informed that if they performed their prison tasks and gained good conduct marks they would obtain the usual reduction of the sentence.

I am now informed that, instead of being discharged as the end of their sentence, these men have been removed to Wormwood Scrubs prison, and are now told that unless they sign an agreement, which, rightly or wrongly, some of them cannot conscientiously sign, they are to be handed back to the military authorities, who may treat them with the utmost rigour of martial law, and even shoot them as they would military deserters.

Surely this is a gross scandal, and one for which we will stand condemned when the history of this war comes to be written; and the recital of our treatment of conscientious objectors will make future generations of liberty-loving men hang their heads in shame.[12]

The Society of Friends – or Quakers as they are more colloquially known – set up a group in Worcestershire, chaired by Richard Cadbury, to provide support to conscientious objectors. The group sought to help COs with their representation at tribunals and court cases, kept notes on the progress of cases, visited and corresponded with COs, and campaigned against their mistreatment. Through the records of this group we have the stories of numerous county COs and their varied experiences. Two cases will serve to illustrate the very different treatment received.

Ernest Baldwyn, resident of Rainbow Hill Worcester, was a local labour leader and member of Cadbury's CO support group. He was, notes Cadbury, 'the first war C.O. to stand out altogether', and thus felt the full force of an unsympathetic tribunal, legal and military system. He was told to join the non-combatant corps by the local tribunal, given partial exemption by the appeal tribunal on the basis that he applied for work of national importance, and then arrested for not doing so. He was tried at the city police court, fined and handed over to the military. But that was not the end of the matter, even though Cadbury paid his fine. He was then court-martialled twice for failing to obey military orders and jailed. The press report of his first court martial highlights the problem of a CO once handed over to the military.

Asked if he wished to call evidence, defendant said he had witnesses whom he could call to speak as to his conscientious objection. The President replied that he was not being charged with anything to do with his conscience. If he disputed being a soldier that was another matter.

Accused: I am not a soldier yet.

The President: You became a soldier automatically under the Military Service Act.

The accused, in a statement read by the court, set out his conscientious objection …

The military had captured his body, and they could do as they thought best with it. 'I shall withhold from you my energies, and my soul you will never have.' He asked the Court to consider his case from this standpoint, and if they agreed, to recommend him for discharge.

In conclusion he expressed regret for causing the military so much trouble. 'My position I cannot help and it is the last of my thoughts to appear insolent or abusive.'

The President observed that the accused had better disabuse his mind of any appeal to the Court. They were there to adjudicate on his offence.[13]

Baldwyn got a year in Exeter jail and after the war put his experience to use as a campaigner for penal reform.

Harold Wrigley, an architect and son of the Unitarian minister at Lye, clearly found a great deal more public support for his stand and that of other objectors, as the *Advertiser* reported on 1 April 1916:

Harold Wrigley in 1911.

Lye Conscientious Objectors
Tribunal sits until after Eleven o'clock
Extraordinary interest

The Lye Tribunal under the Presidency of Mr. J. H. Perry, on Monday sat from five o'clock until a few minutes past eleven, most of the time being occupied in hearing appellants who objected to military service on conscience grounds. Extraordinary public interest was evinced in the proceedings, the Council Chamber in which the meeting was held being crowded with members of the general public, while many people – owing to the large attendance – were unable to gain admittance. Many present appeared to forget the rules which govern a judicial court, and eventually Major Trinham [the military representative] had to protest against the applause which greeted a statement by a conscientious objector. 'It is an insult to the military,' he said, 'and would not be

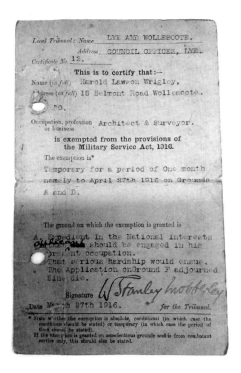

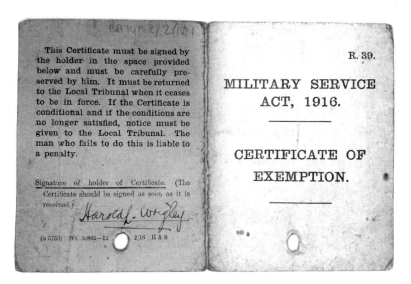

Harold Wrigley's Temporary Certificate of Exemption from Military Service.

allowed in a court of justice.' The chairman then intimated that a similar occurrence would be followed by the clearing of the room.[14]

Wrigley later wrote in 1967 about his experience of the tribunal and its reporting by the press, noting that 'this was in the Spring of 1916. It was reported with much omission from and much addition to what actually happened as I remember it.'

The question that was put to me by the Military Representative at the Tribunal was 'You are not prepared to go and resist this Evil?' I said I had not intended to quote the Bible but he had put the words into my mouth. In short no opportunity was given to question the accuracy of the press statement which [had] obviously been given to the press privately.[15]

Of his subsequent experiences, and the unexpected education that being a CO provided for him, he wrote,

I was given 3 months to wind up my affairs and at the expiration of this time I was offered and accepted alternative service after interviewing the Pelham Committee at Bridge St. Westminster and worked as a farm and market garden labourer for the next 6 or 7 years. It is perhaps superfluous to wonder what I would have done if given no alternative at my first Tribunal. I may have gone to jail – however the passage of that 3 months brought some tolerations to the public mind and to Tribunal members and I had no objection to help grow food. The men who fought did so in accord with their consciences and their sense of what was the only response possible to the German threat, and they had to be fed!

So it came about that on Sept 3rd 1916 I started my land work at Salts Farm, Lancing. Messrs Pullen Berry of Sompting being the employers, who ultimately employed on their various gardens some 15 or 20 C.Os. These C.Os. came from many parts – Wales was represented, 4 of us from the Birmingham area, 1 from Huddersfield and most of the others from the London area.

His fellow COs came from a number of different areas and were of different religious and political persuasions. They included members of the Church of England, Methodists, Salvation Army Institutional Agnostics and Socialists. He was the only Unitarian but there were also were Seventh-day Adventists and Christadelphians. They spent their evenings taking long walks, visiting the house of a local Friend and earnestly debating their various positions on war, socity and life. Of the agricultural labourers he remarked,

The labourers with whom we worked were gentlemen – indeed my 6 years on the land left me with a great respect and admiration for the land workers. I can endorse all that A. G. Street says of them in his book 'The Gentlemen of the Pasture' they accepted us without the bitterness and with the toleration characteristic of those who live to create. They taught us to use spades and hoes, pitchforks, trim hedges, to plough (though not in my case) and to milk cows: indeed I finished on the land as a cowman …

Afterwards I worked near Worcester, in Childswickham, in Bristol and again at the same farm near Worcester and after the War at Melton Mowbray and Ross-on-Wye. But that 4 months in Sussex were memorable to me. That free fellowship of 20 or 30 men all so different and all so genuine was a revelation to me of what men could be when released from the prisons in which so many spend their lives – the prisons of class – the prison of creed – and all the inhibitions natural to the environment into which one is born.[16]

7

The Home Front

The experience of life on the home front during the First World War changed dramatically as the conflict progressed and deepened. From a country where individuals had little recourse to the state unless they were in dire need, Britain transformed itself, for the duration of the war at least, into a nation where the state played a major part in everyone's life. By 1918 the government sought to mobilise human, productive and economic resources in the systematic prosecution of Total War. This came about gradually but with increasing force across the four and a quarter years of conflict. From the initial recruitment drives for the armed forces, attention then fell on expanding the supplies of munitions, then the need for raw materials and foodstuffs, managing the whole labour force, mobilising the country's wealth, controlling consumption and the welfare of the population as a human resource. By the end of 1918 few parts of life were untouched by the state, and all this was set against a backdrop of constant fear and concern for loved ones in military service.

Initially the business of war was left to the professionals and the exhortation was to maintain 'business as usual' while supporting a massive recruitment drive for the armed forces. The concern, at first, was about the hardship war would cause to family and industry because of the disruption in production, trade and family income. There was a reduction in the purchase of many luxury items; the *Kidderminster Shuttle* newspaper, just before war broke out, reported in its regular column on the carpet trade that, 'The fear of a European outbreak of hostilities is sure to have a retarding influence on local industries'[1] By its next edition, on 8 August, Britain was at war and the sober tone of the editorial contrasted with the more excitable tone of the local report:

Editorial

The terrible calamity of war is upon us. A few months since and the statement that our peace-loving, democratic government would be involved in a European war would have been laughed at … The thoughts of every man now should be how best he can serve his country … A town's committee should be formed to concert measures of relief, against the time when the pinch of poverty becomes sharper, and to assist in finding useful work for so many as possible.

Local news

Locally this has been an exciting week, recalling all the stirring scenes witnessed at the outbreak of the Boer War … For the first few days there was a heavy run on the local grocers and provision dealers, housewives being anxious to lay in a good store of provisions. At some establishments stocks were cleared out, and orders were refused. There is no need for any fear with regard to the nation's food supply … Housewives are counselled to exercise care and economy.[2]

On the first day of war, a cabinet committee on the prevention and relief of distress was established and a National Relief Fund followed. A 'Local Representative Committee for the Prevention and Relief of Distress occasioned by the War' and 'Worcestershire Relief Fund' were established, led inevitably by J. W. Willis Bund, chair of the county council, and they immediately requested 'the names and addresses of the persons who have gone on service from each Parish in the County and also those of the homes they have left as by the absence of the men the relations may be placed in altered circumstances'.[3] This massive data collection process proved unmanageable; the information, where it was collected, was out of date before it was returned and no individual cases requiring support were identified through this process. This did not mean that there were no issues or problems; a county council note at its meeting on 14 December 1914, on the work of the committee, states:

So far there has been little acute distress in the committee's area ... At Redditch a considerable number of girls who work in the fishing tackle trade were on short time, and it was apprehended that acute distress might arise. A scheme for establishing a work room will, if necessary, be set up by the Central Committee on Women's Employment ... At Stourbridge several factories are working short time and it is feared that this may cause a need for help. At present such need has not arisen ... At Stourport considerable distress has arisen owing to the factories running short time. A scheme to establish a workroom here has been sent to the Central Committee on Women's Employment, and it is hoped it will get to work ... Under instructions of the Local Government Board a scheme of relief works has been drawn up. It will provide employment should it be found necessary to do so in various parts of the County. [The proposal was to bring forward public works and road building programmes.]

In considering the position of the County as to distress, two matters have to be borne in mind:– 1. The large number of able-bodied men who have joined the army. Probably few counties have sent a greater proportion of recruits in regard to its population than Worcestershire ... As nearly as can be calculated the number of recruits from the present County is 13.5% of the *available* male population ...

The absence of so large a number of the male population will be felt should there be a hard winter, and it is quite possible that there may be considerable distress. It is true that the Government separation allowances go some way to meet this. But the difficulties in the way of providing employment for women in the country districts during the winter months is one that is beset by difficulties ... It will be of interest to state that the Pension Committee has received up to December 5th 424 applications for allowances, and of these 291 were passed at once.[4]

A clear imperative to provide support came with the arrival in the county of refugees from Belgium. Approximately 250,000 spent some time in Britain, arriving via the main population centres and then being housed across the country. They were one of numerous groups, including Irish migrant workers and German prisoners of war, who came to Worcestershire during the war. The arrival of small groups of refugees and the task of providing them with accommodation were regular features in the local news in the autumn of 1914. For example,

A party of 15 refugees have been housed in Droitwich ... The members of the party were people of social standing in their own country. Mr Stanton Ferry of the Royal Hotel is the host of some of them, and the others are accommodated in similar pleasant quarters in the town.[5]

On 17 September, the paper reported,

The family of Father Lambert, private chaplain to Mr R. V. Berkeley of Spetchley Park (consisting of his father, mother and brother and sister) who were recently brought over to England from Malines have been provided with a furnished house at Spetchley by Mr Berkley.

The Mayor is today forming a committee in response to the Government's request to make provision for the Belgium refugees locally. Already many offers of hospitality have been received ... One of the difficulties likely to be encountered by those responsible for the arrangements is the fact that refuges come in families and there is a disinclination for them to separate ... However it is to be hoped that this difficulty will be overcome and that after the families have remained together in Worcester for a few days they will not mind separation.[6]

Lavinia Talbot, staying with her family at Hagley Hall, writes about the arrival of refugees in her diary on 22–23 September 1914.

The 5 Belgium's are very nice and adjustable people ... Mary likes and depends on one of them in her arranging things for the lot who are to be put up in the village ... went to Birmingham w[ith] Mary, Rachel and the nice Belgian girl ... Mary is to bring 12 to a very nice house lent by a young lady in Hagley. A very distressing sight the refugees about 100 men, women and children w[ith] their little bundles of clothes in cloths or petticoats – not a basket or box to be seen ...

The men struck me as the most forlorn and 'out of it' so mixed up and lonely. No one can talk Flemish so the process is difficult to sort out and distribute the poor things. There are numerous homes offered all over England. Mary got hold very luckily of a party ... some of them talk a little French – 12 mostly relations including a Fr [Father] mother and 6 children for Hagley. What desolation it means – and my anger and hate at the Kaiser and his school was burning ...

The 12 turned up in an omnibus, and E and I saw them begin to settle in this new tidy little house. Food ready etc. and kind ladies about. The difficulty is the language and getting work for the men, specially without putting competent English out of work.[7]

The arrival of the refugees sparked anti-German feelings in Britain, particularly as it was accompanied by exaggerated myths and rumours of atrocities committed by the German Army. The majority of the refugees were Catholic and sought Catholic homes for themselves or their children. Most of those working on the numerous local committees to assist refugees were middle or upper class and consequently they often segregated refugees along class lines. Those from middle-class Belgian families were treated rather better, while some refugees were housed in workhouse accommodation. Most refugees spoke Flemish and the language issue did create some problems. In October another report noted that

a party of Belgium refugees are expected in Worcester tomorrow.

About sixteen people are expected, and they will probably be the better class who speak only the Flemish language. They will be comfortably housed at St Catherine's Hall ... the house has been comfortably furnished. Two rooms will be set apart for the use of two Belgium Sisters of Mercy, one of who came from Liege, who have been in Worcester for some days giving advice to the local committee and helping in other ways for the reception of their fellow refugees.[8]

By the end of October there were also homes in Martin Hussingtree, Hindlip and Pershore, and in December over 100 Belgian refugees in Malvern. Some settled in the area and a number helped with the harvests in 1915. The county council reported the 'admission of children of Belgian refugees to council secondary schools free of charge' and the appointment of a committee 'for providing occupations for the refugees'.[9]

Meanwhile the county council, like many employers, sought to reassure employees and their dependents in order to encourage recruitment to the armed forces, resolving in September 1914

that all persons in the employment of the Council or of any of its Committees who shall take service under the Crown, involving absence from their duties during the continuance of the War shall be entitled to receive during their absence such sum in lieu of salary as with the sum paid by the Crown will be equal to the salaries they would have been receiving from the Council if they had remained in the Council's service, and that on their return they shall be entitled to resume their appointments[10]

By December 1914 the county council proudly recorded that

the number of staff on Active Service is now no less than 125, made up as follows:

Committee	Officials	Teachers	Workmen	Total
Education	9	33		42
Finance	4			4
Highways	5		43	48
Sanitary	1			1
Police	30			30
Totals	49	33	43	125

By March 1915 this number was up to 152. The Shirehall had also provided use of its courtyard for parade and the large hall for wet day drill, education and recreation. The council noted, 'This has been greatly appreciated by the men, as is shown by their most excellent behaviour. No annoyance or interruption to business of any kind has occurred.'[11]

As the first rush to the colours subsided, the recruitment calls continued unabated and became shriller. For example, in January 1915 Walter Cheesewright, recruiting organiser for the twenty-ninth recruiting area, Guildhall Recruiting Office, wrote to all shopkeepers in Worcester:

Dear Sir or Madam,

I think you will agree with me that in the present crisis it is the duty of all classes of the community to come to the aid of their King and Country. No class has done more than the employer of labour, and knowing their strong feeling of patriotism I have no hesitation in asking for their support and help.

I am writing to all the shopkeepers of the City of Worcester asking them if they will kindly assist our recruiting Campaign by posting the enclosed Bill on their front window, on Saturday morning next, January 30th, at 10 o'clock.

I have had a variety of Bills printed for this purpose, and every shop in a given area will be posting a different Bill.[12]

One of these bills has become infamous as an indication of recruiting rhetoric taking a step too far:

MOTHERS! YOUR DUTY IS CLEAR
Persuade Your Sons to ENLIST
AT THE GUILDHALL RECRUITING OFFICE, 42, HIGH ST,
WORCESTER

As the war progressed, industries adapted their production to fit in with the war effort; some Kidderminster carpet manufacturers, for example, began to produce army blankets. It became clear that the anticipated shortage of work was quickly being replaced by a shortage of labour; as early as June 1915 the county council reported,

Munitions of War and Labour

An inspector of the Local Government Board on the 23rd April interviewed the Chairman and Clerk of the Council and Surveyor on the subject of a letter addressed by Lord Kitchener on the 31st March to the President of the Local Government Board stating that his Lordship was trying to augment the supply of fitters, mill-wrights, machine hands, and skilled or unskilled labour for use in increasing the output of munitions, and inquiring whether Local Government Authorities had any such persons in their employ who could be taken from them for the vital necessity of the armament manufactories.

Your Committee informed the Board that they were prepared if necessary to release 50 men for the purpose mentioned.

About 60 of the men until recently employed by the Council on the roads have enlisted or left the County for Military purposes.

It was intended during the present financial year to postpone from time to time as much work as possible on the roads so as to enable as many men as possible to be released for Military and farm work.[13]

In May 1915 Asquith was forced, by scandals over claims of a shell shortage at the front, to form a coalition government and appoint Lloyd George as the first Minister of Munitions to co-ordinate industrial production in support of the war effort. However, the introduction of military conscription in January 1916 exacerbated labour shortages and created tensions between the demand for military recruitment and the needs of local industries and small businesses. The newspaper reports and records of debates at military tribunals, frequently discussed in terms of the few conscientious objection cases they heard, are at least as important for the insight they provide into work and family life on the home front. The cases represented the areas from which they came; many in the Evesham, Pershore and Martley areas concerned the challenges of keeping small agriculturally related businesses and market gardens productive as growing numbers of men were called up. In the city of Worcester and north-east of the county the concerns were more industrial, and some reveal the frustrations of employers and workers alike over the vagaries of the Military Service Acts and tribunal decisions. A report of the Worcester Appeals in the *Advertiser* on 1 April 1916 included, among others, these examples:

A Fish Dealer

Mr. W. Stanley Mobberley represented a Stourbridge fish dealer, who is also a common carrier, which was a certified occupation. Appellant was exempted until May 3rd.

Appeal Allowed

A partner in a large coal concern asked for total exemption. Mr. W. Waldron, who supported the claim, mentioned the appellant's firm was supplying munitions works, etc. with fuel. The Military Representative said he wanted to be quite fair and he thought the appellant came under an official order (produced). The appeal was allowed.

No German Wanted

Mr. H. Neild Collis appeared for a Stourbridge confectioner who asked for exemption on the grounds that he was in a certified occupation (bread baker). He also pleaded exceptional business responsibilities. The local tribunal reported that they had formed a very strong opinion that the appeal was formed to avoid military service.

Mr. Collis: Have you advertised in trade journals for a foreman?
Appellant: Yes.
Did you get any applicants?
Yes.
Mr. Collis: How many did you get?

One, but he was a German and I wouldn't have him (laughter). The appeal was refused.

Grocer's Appeal

A Stourbridge master grocer, single, who pleaded various responsibilities, was given till May, and refused leave to appeal.

A Widowed Mother

Another Stourbridge man pleaded that domestic hardship would result if he was called up. His widowed mother was the stewardess at a club in the district, and the appeal was dismissed.[14]

Applicants were often granted exception for a few weeks or months to get their affairs in order or train up a replacement. But this too was contested at the Worcester Appeal Tribunal:

Porcelain Works Cases

The Worcester Porcelain Company applied on behalf of William Hardman (37). Mr. Solon, the managing director, said Hardman was the only man in the works competent to grind and fit ware, and if he went it would deprive many people of work. Seventy-six percent of those eligible had enlisted or had taken up munition work. In reply to Lieut. Glanfield, Mr. Solon said Hardman was passed for general service. The man was engaged in a highly-skilled occupation, and it would be difficult to replace them. Conditional.[15]

Another appeal was put in by the same firm on behalf of John Walter Sedgley, flower painter, the only man left out of ten doing this class of work. 31 October:

Robert O'Callaghan (29), employed as a slip maker at the same works, put in a personal appeal, on the grounds that he was the sole support of a widowed mother. He also stated that he wished to protest against the unfair method adopted by Mr. Solon against him by substituting him for someone else in a department where several men were kept.

Lieut. Glanfield: The Local Tribunal were under the impression that applicant was in a certified occupation, and withdrew the certificate when they found out it was not so. Dismissed.[16]

Writing to the Redditch Tribunal on 2 March 1917, the manager of the Birmingham Small Arms plant in Redditch could hardly contain his exasperation at a recent decision:

Dear Sir,

One of our employees, Edward Johnson, 36 Mount St. Redditch, has brought to our notice a certificate of conditional exemption.

This man is engaged on Military work and we notice under your signature he is to obtain, within 7 days, work on Munitions, or other work of essential National importance, which you specifically state should be in the needle and fish hook trade. Do we understand that it is more essential for this man to be engaged in the fish hook and needle trade than on purely Military work, Yours faithfully, The Birmingham Small Arms Co. Ltd.[17]

Needle and fishing tackle manufacturers did not necessarily fare better. A request from Guillaume Ltd, dated 23 January 1917, as follows, is noted 'Refused'.

Sir, We beg to be allowed to appeal, for John Styler of 275 Beoley Road, formerly a Master Bricklayer, but now entirely in our employ since January first, as muffle builder and Bricklayer. This man is passed for C2 – and obtained Exemption before the Redditch Military Tribunal up to December 31st last as final, applied to you for permission to appeal again but was refused …

We should not have made this application to you if it were not that we are seriously involved in extending our place to be able to cope particularly with Orders from the WAR OFFICE and also to fill Export Orders (when the facility is left to us) … These Orders, particularly those for France and Italy, were before the War supplied by Germany and we wish to be ready to face the competition when it starts again.[18]

Tribunals were the products of the counties in which they operated, sensitive to the needs of particular industries and people of influence in those counties. On 22 March 1916 the forty-year-old single chauffeur of Lord Coventry applied for exemption from military service. Lord Coventry was at this time Lord Lieutenant of Worcestershire and, the committee noted, as he was getting elderly, his nerves were a little frayed. He could not, the committee felt, easily drive himself to undertake the large number of civic and charitable duties that he engaged in on three or four days a week. Yet the committee was split over what to do. One member pointed out that

they must not let it be said that they had one law for Lord Coventry and one for the tenant farmer. He contended that they had a public duty to perform and he didn't intend to deviate from it a bit.

Mr Treherne thought it was possible the man was in public service …

Mr Cubberley said he was also opposed the exemption and was afraid if they granted it they would get themselves further into the ditch than they were in …

Nevertheless,

he moved that total exception be granted.

Mr Treherne seconded, because the military authorities were quite willing. He thought he was doing work for the country.

Mr Tilt supported.

Mr Brown said that he held the same opinion but they had to justify their action and not lay themselves open to the charge that they had favoured Lord Coventry.[19]

The contortions of the tribunal as they sought to reassure the public they were maintaining a 'hard line' while exempting a man protected by Lord Coventry are obvious. One of the many meetings that Lord Coventry attended was cross-county consultations on the danger from Zeppelin raids. These 190-foot airships first bombed Britain in January 1915 and they quickly gained a significant place in the popular imagination as objects of both fear and fascination. The damage caused to buildings by bombing was a visual signifier of Germany's military power and the threat the 'enemy' posed. Never before had civilians been the targets of war. Local newspapers carried extensive reports of raids that had occurred across the country with photographs of the damaged buildings, letters frequently referred to them, and Zeppelins were nicknamed baby-killers, adding to the demonisation of Germany.

Planning for air raids was undertaken early in the conflict, with discussion of who would have the lead authority in the event of a raid and advice sent to local authorities on how to mark hospitals so they were recognisable from the air. However, this advice became more pertinent to Worcestershire with the Zeppelin raid on Birmingham on the night of 31 January 1916. The county council immediately 'represented to the Home Office that in order to protect life and property the imperative necessity of some responsible authority being authorised to extinguish all lights in case of Aircraft raids.'[20] This resulted in agreement to police a blackout, and public notices were duly produced and circulated.

Not everyone considered the regulations reasonable, however, as this letter to the *Worcester Daily Times* indicates:

LIGHTING RESTRICTIONS

Dear Sir – May I ask if the same person who decided to inflict the recent Zeppelin scare on us is the same one who is responsible for the darkening of the city? Why, I should like to ask, is Worcester – one of the least likely towns in the country to be attacked by aircraft – darkened far more than London, Birmingham, and other big towns? We have been assured that ample warning will be given of the approach of hostile aircraft, and yet the centre of the city, which could be plunged into total darkness in a second, is kept in a

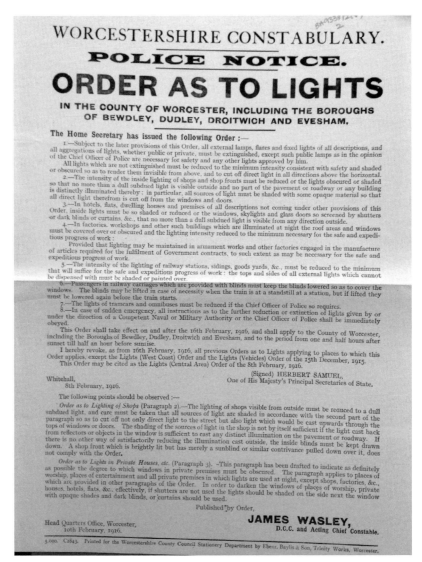

Police notice on street lighting from 1916.

state of positive danger to all who have the misfortune to have to go out after seven o'clock, when the meagre lights from the shops are extinguished.

Why, for instance, should it be necessary to make the centre of the city, where the traffic is greatest and the most lights required, far darker than the suburbs where the same illuminant is used? Before someone is made the wretched victim of a fatal accident, I do hope the authorities will consider the matter and exercise some common sense and discretion.

No one will grumble at the darkening of the gas lights, because they cannot be so easily manipulated in case of immediate danger and the electric current.

While I am on the growl might I suggest that the tramcars should be provided with blinds which could be drawn and so render the cars less conspicuous than they now are, while the lights inside may be restored sufficiently to enable the conductors to see what they are doing, and, at the same time, help to dispel the misery and depression the passengers now have to endure?[21]

Despite this letter, the authorities took the threat of Zeppelins seriously, perhaps because their bombing did not appear to be predictable. The airships were hard to steer and, buffeted by wind, with poor navigation they could not reliably target strategic areas. Arguably, the randomness of the bombing attacks made Zeppelins more intimidating and meant their significance went well beyond the damage they caused. Although few of the residents of Worcester ever saw a Zeppelin, the 'Order as to Lights' was policed with some force, as indicated by examples of prosecutions for lighting offences reported on 7 April 1916, with fines of between five shillings and two pounds, though the magistrates and police showed sensitivity in certain cases.

P. C. Lawley said that in the case of Thomas Martin, of the Locomotive Inn, George Street (who pleaded not guilty), there was a bright light reflected into the street. Defendant said that somebody had turned up the light in the passage. He was fined £1.

Henry Webb, fitter, 23, St. Paul's Street, pleaded guilty. He had a bright light shining from two bedroom windows. Defendant said he had forgotten to draw the blind. He said his wife had had a brother killed and she would not be without a light. The Chief Constable said that as there were hard domestic circumstances he would withdraw the case ...

William Thompson, fishmonger, 33, Shambles, also pleaded not guilty. The Chief Constable said that when the constable went to defendant's shop the defendant abused the constable very badly, and although he had once turned out the light complained of, he turned it on again ... This was the first case under the Order in which he had had to refer to persistent wrong doing ... He was fined £2.

The Zeppelins proved hard to intercept until the introduction of the incendiary bullet in autumn 1916. By this time, Worcestershire was focussed on the huge expansion of government munitions works represented by the establishment of a munitions work in Blackpole.

Production was underway by 1917 but really peaked in 1918, when it was sometimes dispatching nearly 300 million cartridges

Bullet shop at Blackpole Munitions Works in 1917. (With thanks to Worcestershire Archive and Archaeology Service)

a week. As a munitions works it was supposed to be secret and has left few records, but the munitions workers themselves were a popular image of the women war workers in the local papers, which also carried reports that the Baptist Women's League were concerned about the munitions girls swearing.[22]

Women munitions workers. From *Berrows Worcestershire Journal*, 1917.

Munitions workers. From *Berrows Worcestershire Journal*, 1918.

The leisure activities of those who worked in munitions continued to cause anxiety, and some local churches provided 'rational recreation' for them. Their opportunities to spend their wages on drink had already been curtailed by government regulations on pub opening hours and the strength of beer, introduced in 1915. Alternatively, the contribution of Kidderminster to the war effort was put on display when, as the *Kidderminster Shuttle* reported,

a considerable number of distinguished journalists representing the leading London dailies, the America, Canadian, Australian and Indian newspapers have been spending some time inspecting the munitions works which exist in the Midland districts, and on Friday afternoon they paid a hurried visit to Kidderminster, where army requisites are being produced at some of the works ...

Mr Cecil Brinton, of Brintons' Limited, chairman of the local Munitions Committee, had made admirable arrangements. He had got together an extensive collection of various articles manufactured by the local firms, which showed to what extent munition work was being locally undertaken and although the visitors were only able to inspect four works – the Long Meadow Mills, Brintons' Ltd., Bradley and Turton's, and the Castle Motor Works – they obtained from the exhibits a good impression of what was locally being done to meet the needs of the army. Of course, military blankets, felt goods, webbing, and the other products of the spinning and weaving loom were largely in evidence, and the visitors were intensely interested in the exhibition.[23]

As the war progressed, so the financial burden of fighting grew, and the mobilisation of the country's wealth became vital. Fundraising for the war effort began from the first day of war with the War Relief Fund, but such activity became much more organised and centralised as the war progressed. For example, the local war relief done by the Plumber's Arms, Redditch, was handed over to the local council:

Feb 25 1915

Dear Sir,

At a meeting of the Plumbers arms war relief fund held on Monday last it was decided to break it up and the balance in hand to be forwarded to the Redditch war relief fund.

I know you are on the committee of same so am enclosing £3-10s-0d ... will you please send me a receipt for same.[24]

Amateur local efforts at raising war relief funds were replaced by local government and then national drives using slick advertising to sell war bonds, as the focus shifted from war relief funds to finally funding the war effort itself. Fundraising reached its peak of excitement with tank weeks across the country. 'Julian' the tank visited Worcester and various other towns around the Midlands in spring 1918. Julian's arrival was trailed in the press with pictures of the war machine, and published letters from 'Julian' to local girls appeared, such as this in the *Kidderminster Shuttle*, 30 March 1918:

Dear Ivy,

I am coming to Kidderminster, on April 15th, for a week, and I want you to save up for then. You have sent my pater £496,371, and you must kindly make it up to quite £500,000 by the time I arrive. I want you to arrange to lend my pater at least a further £100,000 that week, and then when the war is over I will ask YOUR pater's consent and we will get married. The young ladies here are making quite a fuss of me, and they have thrown money at me as they say THE WAR MUST BE WON. I know all the Kidderminster girls are nice, but I hope to remain true to you. I am still selling War Bonds and 15s. 6d Certificates, and as your money can be got back at any time, kindly tell your cousins at Bewdley, Stourport, Bridgnorth, Droitwich, Highley, Alveley, Cleobury Mortimer, Rock, Hartlebury, and Tenbury, to bring their money to me.

Yours as ever, 'Julian'[25]

On 13 April 1918 the paper reported that 'Julian' was coming:

THE TANK WILL ARRIVE ON SUNDAY AND HAVE A CIVIC RECEPTION

There has been no more popular appeal to Kidderminster and district investors, large and small, than the coming of the tank 'Julian'. This mysterious engine of war has excited the imagination and curiosity of everyone, and the town is sure to be crowded during the next week to see 'Julian'. When the tank first came out of the trenches direct to the homes of the British people, it touched the hearts of those whose part it was to remain in England. Wherever it went it was feted; heralded by bands and escorts, and received by civic dignitaries with all the pomp and circumstance of a conqueror. Cheering crowds have thronged along its route, or waited in the dark and early hours for its appearance ...

As an advertising medium the tank can claim to be the most effective method so far devised to popularise the saving and lending movement ... Where it goes the money flows.[26]

So the conduct of war came to touch Worcestershire people's everyday working and leisure lives. The controls employed by the end of the First World War – rationing of food and materials, air-raid warnings and blackouts – would return a few decades later and be more closely associated with another conflict.

Tank week in Worcester. From *Berrows Worcestershire Journal*, 1918.

8

Worcestershire's Role in Wartime Medical Care

The first industrial war, blasting with heavy artillery, machine-gun fire and snipers' bullets, caused both minor and major damage to the minds and bodies of the soldiers who took part in numerous theatres of war. Soldiers required a range of care to reduce the likelihood of the trauma of being wounded becoming fatal. Worcestershire had a role to play in providing medical attention near the battlefield, but particularly in the care and convalescence of those who were shipped back to 'Blighty'. It was not, however, just injuries that took soldiers out of the front line, but also illness and disease, which could range from enteric ones such as typhoid to trench foot, a result of the wet conditions in many trenches which caused feet to swell and become gangrenous and sometimes led to amputation. Badsey doctor Arthur Sladden, who was in the Royal Army Medical Corps in France and Belgium, described to his father some of the problems he faced in a temporary hospital in Belgium in an early letter home written on 14 October 1914.

Wherever we go we ought to be fixed for some time, for a general hospital is not supposed to run about the country as we have done owing to military contingencies. We have a fair amount of enteric but not alarmingly much I hope that surgery work and inoculation together will prevent any such epidemic as prevailed in S. Africa. Inoculation is voluntary and as from George's experience, it may produce considerable temporary illness – you can imagine that it is not always easy to persuade all the men to have it. I was told off to talk to the men here on the subject and at first they were rather backward in coming forwards but I've roped most of them in by now. Experience shows that inoculation reduces the incidence of disease 5 or 6 times and if inoculated people get it, their chances of recovery are much greater. It is getting steadily colder and damper, we are rather the wetter and for that reason above I think a move will be good – rheumatic cases, of which we have many, don't do over well here, and when the sun doesn't come out it is impossible to get the tents dry.[1]

Whether soldiers' fitness for combat was compromised by injury in combat, disease or a combination of both, their recovery, particularly in an era without penicillin, required that the trauma the body had experienced was contained. They needed rest and recuperation, which was facilitated not just by trained doctors and nurses but also by volunteers and communities. Many of the residents of Worcestershire played a role in nursing soldiers back to health.

Since the mid-nineteenth century and the work of Florence Nightingale, there had been attempts to raise the status and professionalism of nursing, yet at the beginning of the First World War there was still no recognised formal state registration of nurses. By the Edwardian era nursing had begun to be seen as a potential career for young women, who undertook training at city hospitals such as Barts in London. With a degree of planning, which suggests some awareness of the possibility at least of impending conflict, in 1909 the British Red Cross and the St John's Ambulance Society founded the Voluntary Aid Detachment. The role of VAD nurses was to provide civilian support in the event of war. It was planned that they would undertake nursing and cooking duties in hospitals, ambulance trains, rest stations, and in the field. Nationwide there were approximately 55,000 VADs by April 1914 (two-thirds of whom were women). They utilised Boy Scouts to assist with their work – the Scouts often acting as wounded soldiers for the VADs to practise on. They undertook a range of roles including packaging bandages and supplies for hospitals near the front. They were not, however, trained as nurses, although as the war progressed their increasing experience enabled them to take on an increasing range of responsibilities.

When war broke out, some philanthropic young women of independent means set off to provide assistance at the front. Four sisters, Madeline and Susan Bromley-Martin, Eleanor Holland-Martin and Anora Russell from Worcestershire in autumn 1914 set up the Hôpital Temporaire d'Arc-en-Barrois, an emergency evacuation hospital serving the French 3rd Army Corps that was housed in a chateau that had been offered to the ladies by the Duc de Penthievre. It provided large rooms, although initially lacked hot water, gas and electricity. These difficulties were quickly overcome, furniture was made by amateur carpenters among the orderlies and with beautiful grounds and an outdoor ward the hospital proved to be a success, quickly expanding from its initial 110 beds to taking 180 patients at a time.[2]

British troops who were unwell or injured on the battlefield would have gone to a field ambulance, which was a mobile medical unit rather than a vehicle. Here they could receive sufficient treatment to enable them to be safely evacuated to a casualty clearing station,

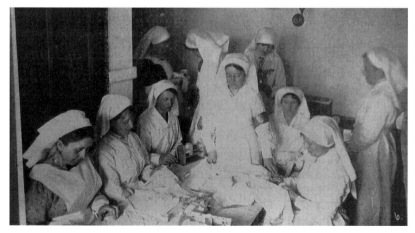

A Worcester Red Cross bandage centre. From *Berrows Worcestershire Journal*, 1917.

a large, fairly well-equipped and static medical facility. The role of these stations was to retain all serious cases that were unfit for further travel; to treat and return slight cases to their unit; and to evacuate all others to base hospitals. Worcestershire soldier Jack described his journey from the casualty clearing station to the base hospital in a letter to his wife on 2 July 1916.

We had a most tedious journey here from the 112th C.C.S. We started at 7:30 a.m. and landed here about 8 p.m. It was a beautiful Hospital train G.W.R with French Engine – each carriage is only supposed to take 40 sitting cases and we were 64. Every carriage was the same – but only the correct number of stretcher cases. When I had been in the train only a few minutes another of our fellows from A Co got in. He was wounded at the same time as I was, a piece of shell caught him on the side of the face knocking some teeth out and cutting his face about badly. His nerves suffered badly and the doctor has put him down for Blighty. I am decked out in Hospital blue with a red tie and can't say I feel much at home in it yet. It is so sloppy somehow, I can hear the guns as I sit here – but not as I <u>have</u> heard them. It is real holiday weather today and there will be something going on in the line if it continues. – I shall be glad to know how Sam and Dick are – I hope you and Libese and the Boy are well – I shall be glad when I get a letter. The sailing vessels out at sea look very nice I wish I was on one.[3]

The base hospital was often a tented camp, although when possible the accommodation would be in huts. Once admitted to a base hospital, the soldier stood a reasonable chance of survival. The physical and emotional trauma of injury often required lengthy nursing care. Nevertheless, Gunner J. Williams of the Royal Field Artillery in a letter to his mother, Mrs W. Abel of Belbroughton near Bromsgrove, presented a cheerful demeanour when he wrote from a hospital in France. The letter was reproduced in *Worcester Daily Times* under a heading of WOUNDED BUT CHEERFUL, as follows:

Just a few lines to let you know that I am still living, and comfortable at present. I am in hospital at — in the North. I believe in France, and quite close to the sea. I received a wound to the face which shut my mouth up for a few days. It has not stopped me from eating now. A shell exploded about 20 yards behind us, and I got a small portion of it into my face and lodged in my chin, but never mind. I can count for a few hundred Germans, as I have pulled the trigger a few hundred times and each shell held 300 bullets, so they should have had a little effect. All the lads are sticking it like heroes. Some of them with fingers and toes blown off are still smiling, I never saw such a cheerful lot. Our battery had all their horses, or nearly all blown to bits about a week ago but got supplied with a fresh lot, but the same thing happened to them. The day I got wounded we had one gun blown to pieces and their sights blown to pieces. Although they got battered about, the Germans could not shift them, and they are still in the same position now, as far as I have heard. They might go forward, but never backward. Good luck to them.[4]

More than half of the soldiers who were injured were sent for further treatment or to convalesce in the United Kingdom, transported there by boat and train as soon as they were considered well enough to make the journey. Victor Godrich of the Worcestershires describes his journey back to Britain in order to recover from trench fever contracted in Gallipoli. He remembered that on 9 January 1916, he

arrived at Spithead on a typical cold, foggy morning after 2–3 days rough passage through the 'Bay'. Everybody on tip-toe anxious to get ashore, but the *Britanic* got into Southampton first and filled all the available trains, so we had to wait on board till the following day when we entrained and were carried us to Whalley Hospital near Blackburn. We had half an hour at Snow Hill Station, Birmingham for tea.[5]

Snow Hill station in Birmingham acted as a junction for many of the hospital trains, but convalescence was rarely arranged close to family or friends. Victor was sent to Lancashire before returning to his regiment in Worcester. Wartime led to many existing British military hospitals being expanded; many civilian hospitals were turned over in full or part to military use. The Worcester Infirmary had thirty beds allocated for soldiers and Stourbridge had a large military hospital.

The arrival of soldiers to Stourbridge made an impact on the local community, which was reported in the local newspaper:

Wounded Heroes
Over 200 Arrive at Stourbridge
Comforts Provided at Town Station
Enthusiastic Reception

Touchingly picturesque, many of them, in their varied and torn clothing, their improvised headgear their halting gait, and many other evidences of devoted and self- sacrificing service, a train load of wounded soldiers – probably the largest contingent of battle broken men ever brought into the township – arrived at Stourbridge Town Station on Wednesday afternoon en route for the Military hospital at Wordsley. They were met by staff officers and by the trained men of the RMC and also by the skilled VAD of local ladies, who supplied them with cheering comforts and generous nourishment before dispatching them on the final stage of their journey. A crowd of hundreds of local residents raised hearty and sympathetic cheers as the heroes passed in motor-cars and motor ambulances on their way to Wordsley.[6]

Soldiers with less serious injuries stayed in auxiliary units and private convalescence hospitals. In Worcestershire there were over thirty opened in large houses and public buildings. One of the first was in Evesham Manor, which the owner, Mrs Rudge, had ready to receive patients in by 24 September 1914. Similarly the Bishop of Worcester turned the college for training clergy at Hartlebury Castle into a VAD hospital. Many other hospitals followed, in Pershore, Malvern, Droitwich, The Larches near

Kidderminster and Battenhall. Officers and men were usually in separate hospitals. Thus many soldiers injured in any of the various fields of conflict spent time in Worcestershire recovering from the trauma. William Townsend wrote with relief to let his family know where he was on 30 September 1915.

Dear Mother,

I have arrived at the Military Hospital at Stourbridge, Worcestershire. I have been wounded in the knee and am going on quite well, it is not very serious so do not be alarmed. I have got to England alright this time. Hoping to hear from you soon. From your loving son, Will.

Stourbridge Town VAD[7]

The number of recovering soldiers who stayed in the Worcestershire hospitals was considerable. More than 3,600 injured servicemen were treated at Evesham Manor Hospital alone. It had a fully equipped operating theatre and dressings ward located in what had once been the conservatory of the imposing house looking over the River Avon.

Evesham Manor hospital during the First World War. (From the private collection of the Rudge family)

VAD and auxiliary hospitals took patients who were generally less seriously wounded than those in the main hospitals and who needed convalescence before returning to active service or being discharged. The VAD hospitals' role was to provide relief and restoration so that not only the patient's body but also their mind could recover from the trauma of injury and the long journey from the battlefront back to the UK. The provision of a good diet, calm, sleep and nursing care were seen as central to this recovery. Massage and physiotherapy was also often available.

Inmates at the Hartlebury VAD hospital wrote about how they got there and of their gratitude for their care in a scrapbook for the commandant and staff. For example Private Spencer of the Second Worcestershire Regiment wrote on 13 June 1915,

I transferred form the Royal Warwicks into the above regiment to keep them at war strength and was wounded at Hitchebourg on the 18 May 1915 whilst volunteering to fetch rations for our company.

Staff and patients at Evesham Manor hospital. From *Berrows Worcestershire Journal*, 1917.

Arrived in England on the 21st May and after a week in Birmingham hospital was sent to this comfortable Convalescent Hospital and after a fortnight of enjoyment left on 13 June 1915. I am very grateful for the benefits I have received and the highest praise I give to the Commandant Sister and nurses alike and shall never finish giving my praises to them as a friend in need is a friend indeed.[8]

Some soldiers had been in the army before the First World War, so their descriptions of their journey leading to Hartlebury go back much further. For G. C. Brooker this was six years and five months, including time in India:

India is a splendid country and I would advise anyone to go there. I came home arriving at Plymouth on the 24 December 1914 for France, going into action on the 25th of January until being taken into the hospital with Frost Bite, during my stay at Hartlebury Convalesce Home, I had a splendid time and was treated with respect. I hope every man staying here will appreciate the kindness they are having and will have during their stay in Hartlebury. Thanking one and all for their great kindness to me.

G. C. Brooker[9]

The allocation of servicemen to hospitals was not linked to their regiments or their homes but was often linked to a larger hospital.

June 28th 1915

I went out to the front on the 9th of February for the second time. I got wounded on the 21st of April at Hill 60. I was sent back to England and I came to Birmingham hospital and from there to Hartlebury. I was here for 6 weeks and enjoyed myself while I was here and I was very sorry to go away, and I hope if I get wounded again they will send me back to Hartlebury

S Hohnson
First Cheshire Regiment[10]

Patients at Hartlebury Castle VAD. (With thanks to Worcestershire Museum Service)

Local Worcestershire women with families and domestic responsibilities and no medical training formed the principal staff of the hospitals. A lead article in the *Worcester Herald* explained,

Those who have not been trained as nurses would not be much good at the front, even if they were able to go, but there are few women who could not give efficient help in a sick room or a ward of a hospital under the supervision of a good trained head. Most, perhaps all, of the members of the Red Cross Society have been through an ambulance course and many have had instruction in nursing and although this does not imply sufficient knowledge to take sole charge it does mean that a women is much better equipped than she would have been without instruction.[11]

The hospitals, which were often administered by the Red Cross, might include the following staff:

A commandant, who was in charge of the hospital (except for medical and nursing services)
A quartermaster, who was responsible for the receipt, custody and issue of articles in the provision store
A matron, who directed the work of the nursing staff
Members of the local Voluntary Aid Detachment (VADs), who were trained in first aid and home nursing
Other volunteers
Paid domestic servants, who might, for example, undertake the cooking.

There are indications that for many middle- and upper-class women these hospitals offered scope to undertake a welcome range of activities and responsibilities outside the private sphere of the home, although in many respects what they were doing was just an extension of their pre-war domestic roles. Work for the VADs in the convalescence hospitals ranged from cleaning and polishing to changing dressings, applying fomentations, and taking temperatures, as the patients were not usually in need of serious medical attention. In nursing, however, middle-class women were liable to come into close physical contact with men and their bodies in ways that they would not normally have done in the pre-war era.

Recovering servicemen were under military control; they had to wear the clearly identifiable blue uniform which marked out their status as wounded combatants. At the Abbey Manor Hospital in Evesham the rulebook made it quite clear that Breakfast was at 8 a.m., Dinner at 12.30, Tea at 5 and Supper at 7.30 p.m. Patients could go out into the town in the mornings and afternoons, but had to return by teatime. Furthermore, after 6 o'clock in the evening the park, woods and roads were out of bounds and patients were restricted to the front of the house, the tennis lawn and the area around the tents. Any man who broke these rules

Mrs Rudge of Evesham Manor hospital and the operating theatre there. (From the private collection of the Rudge family)

would have his pass stopped. The autograph books of Hartlebury VAD hospital suggested that many of the inmates there seemed to find returning by the allotted time rather challenging.

Soldiers' entries in the autograph book at Hartlebury Castle and Battenhall hospitals emphasised how it has been to them a 'home from home'. One inmate explained, 'I can honestly say you could not wish for a better staff that what is here. They are very kind to all of us and I can sincerely say they are doing all they possibly can for me.' Appreciation of the kindness, caring and nurturing appears in almost all the entries. 'I spent a most happy month at the above convalesce home, for which I am most grateful I found the nurses always very kind and anxious to help me when I was sick.'

Peter Stretch, 8th City of London Regiment, Post Office Rifles, also enthused about his period in Worcestershire:

> East or west, home is best
> but at Battenhall let me rest.
> I dreamt I died and to heaven did go
> Where I came from, they wanted to know,
> when I said 'Worcester' St Peter did stare
> But he said come inside you're the first one from there.[12]

Alternatively, Trooper Cowley, 2nd OWH (Queen's Own Worcestershire Hussars) composed the following poem, which was copied into Battenhall's autograph book by Sergeant S. R. Evans of the Rifle Brigade. He had been wounded at Loos on 31 July 1915 and wrote the poem out as 'a small mark of appreciation of the many kindnesses shown us' on 5 January 1916, when he left to return to his unit.

> Battenhall! Battenhall,
> We're all fond of beneath
> take me there when I am ill
> VAD beneath Red Hill
> Battenhall! oh Battenhall

where the sisters are so kind
Oh Oh Oh oh battenhall
by this we are of one same mind.[13]

The autograph books also contain evidence that the soldiers
were full of praise for the kindness they received from the nurses/
VADs; there is a sense that they felt 'mothered' and provided with
home comforts without any home responsibilities, and this they
appreciated. The following little ditty is another written about a
stay in the hospital and stressing the home comforts it provided.

Tho from home I am far away,
At Hartlebury Castle I would stay
if only I did have the chance
and was not needed back in France.
At Hartlebury there is a VAD
who has made a wonderful change in me.

Down at Hartlebury VAD
We got sugar in our tea
Real coal upon the fire we burn
and are given three and six that we don't earn.
So now boys take my advice
and get a blighty for its nice.

There's none can tell unless they've been
Where shell holes are all to be seen,
how grateful wounded tommies are
to all those who tend their needs.
And I for one tend them my thanks
and wish them good luck with all my heart.[14]

Servicemen stayed in the auxiliary and VAD hospitals for a few
weeks or several months; as they got better they were expected
to undertake tasks to ensure the hospitals ran smoothly, perhaps

working as orderlies. They were taken on sightseeing trips and were able to go out of the hospital. Occupations were provided for them, such as sports, amateur dramatics and handicrafts.

The moral and class cultures of the owners, however, shaped permitted behaviour – thus, according to the rule book at Evesham Manor Hospital, 'All patients able to walk into town must of a Sunday go to their places of worship in the charge of an Officer of the House or an Orderly and Non Commissioned officer. There is no leave on Sunday Morning otherwise.'[15] Nevertheless the men tended to prefer the VAD and auxiliary hospitals to the military hospitals as they were less crowded, discipline was more relaxed and the atmosphere more homely.

Victor Godrich, who was in the Yeomanry, remembers his stay in Malvern:

I was taken from there, with others, to Malvern where a 'convalesent home' had been established in the pre-War headquarters of the

Staff and patients at the infirmary in Worcester at an embroidery class. From *Berrows Worcestershire Journal*.

Malvern Squadron. The only officer concerned was an old Major who owned a carpet factory at Kidderminster.

He visited us about once a fortnight but as his factory was busy, he could not spare much time for regimental duties (although he was drawing army pay) ...

We had a visit by a local Sergeant Major two or three times a week. He did not drill us but took us on country walks for exercise. 'We also had a few visits to the Malvern Rifle Range.

Whilst at Malvern, as we were settling down to our comfortable quarters, we also read in the papers that our regiment had suffered terrible disasters at Oghratina and Katia on the Sinai Desert. This occurred on Easter Sunday 23rd April 1916. More than 100 comrades were 'killed in action'.

This put a heavy shadow on our life in Malvern and most of us were anxious to go out again and avenge our old pals. Our move didn't come until October, probably due to shortage of transport.[16]

At Evesham Manor hospital visitors were allowed on Friday and Sunday afternoons until 5 p.m. Relatives could visit at any time between 2 and 6; those that had come a significant distance were often provided with accommodation by the local community, who supported wives and mothers visiting their husbands and sons in the hospital. Thus caring for the wounded extended beyond those who nursed or volunteered in hospitals; farmers donated food to Evesham Manor Hospital. Across the country local communities became involved in the National Egg Collection for the Wounded Soldiers, a scheme that had Queen Alexandra as its patron. Over 2,000 collection points were organised by volunteers, from where eggs were packed into boxes with straw, and shipped to hospitals in France and Britain. Poultry keeping was a predominantly female and rural undertaking but in urban areas women were expected to utilise fewer eggs in their cooking, contributing those saved to the campaign.

Local communities, clubs and workplaces also took on the responsibility of caring for the wounded men in Worcestershire hospitals more directly by organised outings and entertainment for the wounded soldiers. Local residents put on concerts and plays; Hartlebury Hospital autograph books indicate that soldiers went on outings and put on pantomimes for the local community in which they seem to be well integrated. In Evesham the town council placed a number of seats in the town for the use of wounded soldiers only.

Evesham also introduced a canteen in town for all men in uniform and their friends; it proved popular with the inmates from the hospital and soldiers home on leave. The *Evesham Journal* reported its opening on 1 June 1918.

The ladies have been most energetic in fitting up the room in the basement comfortably and attractively. Rugs and carpets are placed on the floors, comfortable easy chairs are placed round small tables, vases of flowers are placed in the windows, a piano has been provided and the somewhat cheerless room in the basement presented quite

A group of munitions workers and wounded soldiers on an outing to Tewkesbury. From *Berrows Worcestershire Journal*, 1918.

a pleasing appearance on Tuesday … Light refreshments will be provided at reasonable charge, newspapers and periodicals available. The reading and magazine rooms at the Public Library will be open and writing materials provided … The wants of the guests were very quickly satisfied by the army of ladies and it was not long before the men were enjoying a smoke, tobacco and cigarettes were being freely distributed.[17]

Many of the social events and activities at hospitals were geared towards raising funds. Whist drives and garden fetes were particularly popular but sporting events – for example between local women's football or cricket teams – were a feature of the county's schedule by 1918. Support for the Red Cross was ubiquitous; it raised 22 million pounds during the war and its mission touched the spirit of the era. Consequently, its annual flag day was called 'Our Day'.

Abbey Manor held a large annual fundraising fete, and in 1918 Frances Rudge wrote to the *Evesham Journal* to explain how the proceeds of the event would be distributed.

Red Cross collectors at a garden fete in Hadzor House. From *Berrows Worcestershire Journal.*

Dear Sir, – with regard to the fete to be held in these grounds on July 24th and 25th will you very kindly allow me to put the following before your readers? With the consent of Headquarters I propose using the proceeds for the following objects: the Abbey Manor Hospital Ambulance Fund, the Worcestershire Branch of the Red Cross Society, the Worcestershire Prisoner of War Fund and Abbey Manor Hospital Fund. My daughter's car and my own have been used for Red Cross work since the beginning of the war and they have hopelessly broken down. I advertised for the loan of a car by the advice of the British Red Cross Society but without success. Mr Tipper very kindly conveyed all the patients to and fro from the station with the help of Mr C Burlingham and Mr G White during the time we went without a car.

With 145 beds an ambulance was urgently needed and Sir E. M. Clarke, Director of the Motor Ambulance Department, took the matter in hand, with the result that a 1916 Overland Chassis was brought and fitted with an ambulance body under the supervision of the Red Cross engineer at a total cost of £325. I have received so much sympathy and help from the people of Evesham and the district during the last three years that I confidently ask them for their help to pay for the ambulance or to give me donations for which ever object appeals to them most. We have had 1,900 patients, and I think your readers will be interested to know that with the exception of the ration money for the men, I have never received any money from the British Red Cross Society, or from any other source for this hospital, and it has been kept up entirely by generous help given by the public.
Faithfully yours
Florence Haynes Rudge
Auxillary hospital
Abbey Manor
Evesham
June 16 1918[18]

In the spring of 1918 plans for the great offensive on the Western Front were laid, and experience had taught that casualties were

Evesham Manor's motorised ambulance, acquired in 1918. (From the private collection of the Rudge family)

likely to be of epic proportions. All hospitals were urged to increase the number of beds available, and Florence Haynes-Rudge took the tenancy of Chadbury House and converted it into an annexe to Abbey Manor, thus adding a further 45 beds. Some soldiers were no longer able to fight after their stay in hospital, while others had several periods of injury or illness over the course of the war. There are also newspapers cuttings in the autograph books kept by the Commandant at Hartlebury Castle VAD hospital which report the subsequent deaths of former inmates of the Worcestershire convalescence hospitals.

9

Famous Faces of Wartime Worcestershire

In addition to the thousands of Worcestershire people who gave their lives or who returned, perhaps wounded either physically or mentally, from the war, a number of individuals who made their mark in other ways had Worcestershire connections. These included the women, children and older men who worked the land and local industries, and the heroes. Some, like Private Dancox, became known for heroic exploits. Fred Dancox, born and bred in Worcester, served in the 4th Battalion Worcestershire Regiment through the war. He was awarded the Victoria Cross for action at Poelcapelle on 9 October 1917. Dancox overcame a German block-house single-handedly, running from one shell hole over to another before getting into the block-house, threatening the occupants with a grenade, taking them prisoner and bringing them back to British lines. Additionally he retrieved the machine gun that had been causing such havoc on his comrades in the attack.[1] When it was rumoured he was due on leave on 1 December, *Berrows Journal* reported the crowds and bunting that awaited him in Dolday:

On Wednesday afternoon, lines of people gathered in the city's streets, all waiting to catch a glimpse of the soldier. Workmen suspended operations to hang about factory and workshop doors, and girl clerks pushed up windows and peered forth. Noisy and eager crowds also thronged Shrub Hill Station.[2]

What was particularly poignant was that Ellen Dancox, who had last seen her husband twelve months previously, was soon to learn that Fred had been killed at Cambrai on 30 November. For his mother, Louisa Whittle, Fred was the fourth of her four sons to be killed that year.

At the other end of the social scale was Jack Lyttelton. In common with others in the gentry, Lyttelton was an officer in the Yeomanry before the war and a veteran of the South African campaign. He was elected as MP for Droitwich in 1910 but relinquished it in 1916, by which time it was clear his duties in the war prevented him from acting for Droitwich. In September 1915 he wrote a 'catching-up' letter to his wife, Violet, detailing life in Egypt and then contrasting it with the sudden change when joining the fighting in Gallipoli:

I do not know that you have had any sort of clear history of our movements & doings since the palmy days of Alexandria & my letters have all been of a somewhat sketchy nature owing to very adverse circumstances & conditions for letter writing. On or about the boys birthday [8/8] we won the Inter-Regimental Polo tournament in Cairo – a great event & the finest fun. A massive cup became the property of the Regiment for a year by this victory & we had just time to get the Regiment's & our names inscribed on the shield & to drink success to ourselves out of it when we set sail for the Dardenelles. We were an odd crowd. From being, so we fancied, a somewhat dandy cavalry Regiment we suddenly found ourselves transformed into most unbecoming infantry, loaded with heavy infantry equipment with piles of ammunition and entrenching tools.[3]

Later in the same letter, Lyttelton reported on the Yeomanry's landing and attack at Suvla Bay:

A big bombardment by our guns howitzers, field batteries & naval guns on ships shifted a good deal of the landscape in the morning, but probably did not do much else …

We moved off on our beautiful array & the first thing that happened was that we were caught under concentrated shrapnel fire, beautifully burst, at fairly close range by a Turkish battery of 6 guns. This was unexpected, for though many of us knew that that particular spot was a favourite object of the Turkish gunners attention & that they had the range to a nicety, having watched through our glasses many an exciting little episode on previous days occurring there, yet we were told either the Turkish batteries would be knocked out by this morning's bombardment, or, if not, that their attention would be so much occupied elsewhere, that they would not turn their guns on us. We (that is the wise ones) however knew we should be in for it there. And we were right.

One of the 'little episodes' referred to above, was a small party of 2 men and 4 horses going across this particular open space down to water. A Turkish observer spotted them, & the battery having nothing better to do, turned on them one gun. It made perfectly beautiful shooting & killed one of the horses. Now we had to pass close to that dead horse, so we – that is, the 3 officers, Leslie Cheape, Hugh Cheape & myself – who had watched it killed from the hill two miles away, knew more about it than the others, who fancied our march as safe as Rotten Row. It was an exciting & thrilling 20 minutes before we were again in comparative safety, but alack! We left between 700 & 800 of our fine division knocked out behind us. We set out about 4,500 strong. After a ten minutes breather we again set out to assault some hill or hills, which nobody seemed very clear about. For the rest of the day we were under fairly hot rifle and machine gun fire, which did not do us a great deal of damage. We moved this way and that, supported this unit & that unit with fine impartiality, until at nightfall we found ourselves in the front line ready to do or die again in the morning, but the men were pretty tired. However that was not to be, for at 2 am in the morning we suddenly received orders that the 2nd Mounted Division would withdraw into support.

A couple of months later Jack was back in Egypt, working at the HQ of the Mediterranean Expeditionary Force and somewhat more reflective about the cavalry's experience. On 24 November 1915 he wrote home:

The Regiment have been here [Alexandria] for a fortnight & are now embarking to return to their horses in Egypt. I stay on here for goodness knows how long, I do not think to return is as attractive compared to the job I am now employed on, which is of great interest & although perfectly safe, is taking a hand in the big game. The season in Egypt with its racing & polo would seem tasteless & out of place after what we have been through especially August at Suvla Bay.[4]

He went on to command the Yeomanry Regiment. He was to succeed his father as the 9th Viscount Cobham in 1922. He was Undersecretary of State for War in Neville Chamberlain's government between 1939 and May 1940, and Lord Lieutenant of Worcestershire from 1923 to 1949.

Another large and influential family closely associated with the county was the Cadbury family of Quakers and chocolate manufacturers. The Cadburys had a mixed engagement with the war for, despite their Quaker beliefs, one of the sons, Major Egbert Cadbury, was awarded the DSC for shooting down two Zeppelins. The head of the family, George Cadbury, who was one of the leaders of the Peace Society and had his family home in Bournville, Birmingham, removed the family to Malvern for much of the war. His nephew Richard Cadbury was a resident of Rose Hill, Worcester, and a strong advocate of Quaker beliefs in the immutability of personal conscience and the broader Liberal cause in Worcester throughout this period. It must have been with great sadness that Richard Cadbury felt he had to resign his vice presidency of the Worcestershire Liberal Council in 1916 in response to the Liberal-led coalition government's introduction of conscription, though it elicited this respectful reply on 22 May 1916.

Dear Mr Cadbury,
Your wish to withdraw your name during the war from the list of vice presidents of this council was communicated to the Executive at

their meeting on Saturday. I was instructed to say that they received it with sincere regret, remembering your valued support during many years past, and that they trust it will not be long before in happier circumstances you are able to resume cooperation with your old political friends in the cause of freedom and progress which they know you have at heart. Yours sincerely, W. G. R. Stone.[5]

The following letter dated 5 June 1917 from Uncle George indicates not all Quakers felt their consciences demanded complete refusal to co-operate in the war effort:

My dear Richard,

I am enclosing £5 as last year, towards the Mission Van Work in the Villages and Hop Fields in the neighbourhood of Worcester.

We have closed the Manor House and are living at Malvern, just running over to Bournville for two or three days each week. We are generally away on Tuesdays and Wednesdays – sometimes Thursdays – but any other day if you are in our neighbourhood, we should be delighted to see you to afternoon tea.

We had a few lines from Jessie a day or two ago. She seems very busy preparing surgical bandages, etc. for the army. Our thoughts, as you may suppose, are often turned towards Bertie – who is following the most dangerous of all callings, belonging to the Royal Naval Air Service, and Laurence – who a fortnight ago received from the French government the Croix de Guerre for his brave work in rescuing French wounded – and Molly – who is having a fairly strenuous time of it in hospital work at Dunkirk.

With love to Carrie, your attached uncle, George Cadbury.[6]

However, Richard Cadbury clearly took the view that his conscience demanded that he refuse to cooperate with the war effort in any way and he did not shy away from making this clear both locally and nationally, for example, in this response to the Mayor of Worcester and City of Worcester National Service Committee:

March 29 1917

I have received the papers regarding national service. – I am sorry I cannot see my way to signing it. With me it is a matter of conscience. I <u>cannot</u> serve two masters. I have since I came to Worcester put time and money to the things which I believed would best serve both God and man. I have and am still doing my best. I have no right as a Christian to place my own free conscience in the hands of another, to dictate what I shall or shall not do.

I am rearing goats, growing fruit, vegetables, potatoes. What land I cannot myself cultivate I have let in allotments. My mission in Friar St may not be thought much by others, but it is the work God has given me to do, and as long as I am free I intend to support it. My coffee house takes too a considerable part of my time.

Both mission hall and coffee house have done every moral work to help the nation in a <u>gentle</u> way, under the present circumstances, then I have immeasurable private, public and semi/public responsibilities. Last night I was 'at it' from 7.30am to 11.30pm so I don't think I can be said to be shirking work.[7]

The following letter was in response to a circular letter from the Chancellor of the Exchequer.

July 6th 1917

The Rt. Hon. A. Bonar Law M.P.
Dear Sir,

Your circular letter regarding war loan to hand, seems to demand a reply.

Granted that – humanly speaking – the war was inevitable, was it not so, largely as the result of our unholy alliances in the past, – unholy partly because of the selfish ends, unholy because of the result of suspicion, which raised suspicion, which again intensified suspicion.

But even granting that under the circumstances this nation had to fight, one other question must dominate, – I am a Christian, can I as a Christian take up arms. – I have studied the New Testament, and have tried to do so without bias, and can only come to the conclusion, that according to the life and teachings of Jesus Christ I cannot do so. And this being the case I cannot logically, or wilfully help others to do so.

There is another side of the question which appeals to me, – and I think that the more who will give their views on the subject can only help those who govern, to come to a right conclusion in the matter. – A ruined country can never be said to have won any battle, and whatever maybe the success of this war loan. – If I read the times aright, there opens out a future for this country of such ruin and dislocation, such poverty and misery, such as it has never know, – and as I love my country, and thank God for a King whom I believe to be thoroughly good at heart; – I long to see this country stop in its long plunge to ruin before it is too late.

Yours respectfully,
Richard Cadbury[8]

The experiences of some of Worcestershire's cultural and literary figures can also be traced through their writings and activities. Edward Elgar was born and bred in Worcestershire and the county was responsible for much of his inspiration, but he actually spent most of the war in London. As has been described many times, Elgar became concerned and angry that his music was being used to support and promote a war that he increasingly felt was a waste of men's lives. Although we may now associate some of his most popular music with the martial Edwardian air, it was his religious music that featured most highly at the time. The Coles brothers had some contact with him in 1916 and Cecil Coles of the Queen Victoria Rifles wrote asking Elgar to correspond with his wounded brother John, whose copy of the 'Dream of Gerontius' was by then 'lying in the Mametz Wood where he had been wounded'. He explained that this brother had

carried a copy of the poem and the vocal score into the trenches with him, and has delighted souls by playing the music to them, sometimes with the help of a fellow violinist in the regiment.[9]

Elgar obviously did write to John because his reply reads:

Dear Sir Edward Elgar, it was with very great pleasure that I received your very kind letter some time ago. I have quite recovered from my wounds now and am discharged from Hospital. I was lucky to get my Active Service Copy! Of the Gerontius music sent home so I am able still to enjoy it[10]

While John went on to receive a commission in 1917, Cecil, a talented composer himself, was killed in April 1918 while carrying wounded back to the lines and is buried at Crouy-sur-Somme.

The famous Victorian poet A. E. Housman was born near Bromsgrove. He rose to fame with the publication of his collection of pastoral poems entitled *A Shropshire Lad* in 1896. He extolled the beauty of not merely Shropshire but also of the county of his birth, Worcestershire, and particularly Bredon Hill. In the bucolic culture of the First World War the poems became increasingly popular and in 1917 his poem in praise of the 'Old Contemptibles' (British Expeditionary Force) of 1914 was published in *The Times*.

Epitaph on an Army of Mercenaries
These, in the day when heaven was falling,
The hour when earth's foundations fled,
Followed their mercenary calling
And took their wages and are dead.

Their shoulders held the sky suspended;
They stood, and earth's foundations stay;
What God abandoned, these defended,
And saved the sum of things for pay.

One of the most interesting literary links with the county comes by accident. Vera Brittain, author of *A Testament of Youth* among other books and mother to Dame Shirley Williams, was engaged to Roland Leighton, himself a writer, who joined the 7th Battalion, Worcestershire Regiment. He had enlisted in the Norfolk Regiment in November 1914 and sought leave to join his friend and Vera's brother, Edward Brittain, in the 11th Sherwood Foresters, but in his efforts to be posted to a regiment going to the front, was accepted by 7th Worcestershires sometime in early March 1915. On 1 April he sailed for France.

By August he was already 'depressed and disheartened', writing that 'there doesn't seem anything worth living for'.[11] Newly arrived in France after a week's leave, he recalled the scene days before at Victoria station where the 'men were boisterously cheerful in a manner which deceived no-one'. Perhaps unsurprisingly, Leighton was soon obsessed with the rigmarole of life at the front:

My present consists now of walking long miles of trenches, mostly very muddy and dilapidated and intermittently giving Sunday instructions to unshaven and mud-bespattered followers with a view to the aforesaid ditches becoming ultimately more inhabitable.[12]

On the occasional sunny day he felt it 'a pity to kill people on a day like this' – hastily adding, 'I suppose it is a pity to kill people on any day, but opinions – even my own – differ.'[13] From his letters it is clear that Leighton moved through depression and morbidity to periods of enthusiasm and cheerfulness. In the build-up to the Battle of Loos, his unit 'slept not only in our clothing as always but hung round with revolvers, haversacks etc & ready for an alarm; but it never came'.[14] On 30 November, after a period of snow and cold, rain took over and 'the trenches are half full of liquid mud, suddenly-thawed traverses have fallen and blocked the way with earth and sandbags ... apart from the difficulties of locomotion I enjoy myself thoroughly'.[15] However, that naivety was replaced by reality very soon, as a week or so later he wrote that the trenches were very wet and muddy, and many of the communication trenches are quite impassable. Three men were killed the other day by a dug-out falling in on top of them and one man drowned in a sump hole … One consolation is that the German trenches seem to be, if anything, worse than ours.[16]

So typically of many men, Roland's last letter, a few days later, was brief and expectant: 'Shall be home on leave for week from 24th Dec. – 31st. Land Christmas Day.'[17] He was shot while inspecting the wire on 22 December in front of Hébuterne, died the following day and is buried at Louvencourt Cemetery.

Worcester's most famous daughter, Vesta Tilley, was born as Matilda Powles near Wyld's Lane and grew up to be known as a great recruiting sergeant for the war effort. Vesta was already well known in 1914; married to theatre and film producer Walter De Frece, she had celebrated her fiftieth birthday and she was on the brink of retirement from the stage. She had been performing since she was a child and had toured America on at least two occasions. She was particularly well-known, even before the war, for playing the role of a man on stage, and singing from that perspective, often in uniform.

In her autobiography, she makes little mention of her war work; instead she relates experiences of air raids in London and Brighton. On one occasion, while playing at the London Coliseum, she stayed at the Savoy, where her room faced the Embankment, opposite Savoy Mansions.

The maroons started again, and I saw quite plainly a machine flying overhead. At the same moment there was a terrific exposition and I was hurled across the room as the windows cracked and blew in. Luckily I was not hurt, just bruised … A bomb had dropped on Savoy Mansions, cutting the building clean in two … If the bomb had fallen a few seconds earlier it would certainly have struck the part of the hotel in which my rooms were situated.[18]

Publicity still from Six Days' Leave. (WAAS Vesta Tilley Collection, with thanks to the Worcestershire Archive and Archaeology Service)

Miss Vesta Tilley is selling her photographs for the benefit of the brave men at-the-Front

The money received is devoted to sending 1/- parcels (really 3/6 worth) of tobacco and cigarettes through "The Performer" Tobacco Fund.
And one of these photographs is enclosed in each parcel to liven up a Dug-out.

Will you help to make the men happy?

The more photographs you buy the more cigarettes will be sent, and the more men you will make happy.
As nearly all the leading artistes are selling their photographs through "The Performer" Tobacco Fund, **you can make a souvenir collection** by sending your remittance direct to :—

Hon. Treasurer,
"The Performer" Tobacco Fund,
18, Charing Cross Road,
London, W.C. 2

5/- will buy a collection of **20** artistes
every one different, and post free
10/- will buy a collection of **40** artistes
every one different, and post free
21/- will buy a collection of **100** artistes
every one different, and post free
£5 will buy a collection of **500** artistes
every one different, and post free

"The Performer" Tobacco Fund is a branch of the Newspapers Patriotic Tobacco Fund, which is approved by the War Office and licensed by the War Charities Act, 1916.

For **1/-** we send 'Smokes' that would cost you **3/6** if you bought them in a shop at home

A special arrangement has been made with Martins Ltd., 210, Piccadilly, London, W., to pack and despatch these 1/- parcels duty free from in bond, thereby enabling "The Performer" Patriotic Tobacco Fund to send for 1/- what would cost 3/6 if bought in a shop at home. And the Military Authorities (through the Director General of Voluntary Organisations—Sir Edward Ward) have kindly undertaken to collect and deliver the parcels to the men at-the-Front free of charge

P-438

The reverse of the publicity photo. (WAAS Vesta Tilley Collection, with thanks to the Worcestershire Archive and Archaeology Service)

Vesta experienced a number of air raids while staying on the South Coast, where no lights were permitted at all. 'At Brighton, while playing at the Hippodrome, I was obliged to literally feel my way from Middle Street to the Metropole Hotel each night after the performance.' At Margate she witnessed a daylight raid:

It was a magnificent sight, awe-inspiring to a degree. Our anti-aircraft guns had opened fire as the bombers neared the shore. I saw one of our boys go up in a small machine to intercept the invaders, and his machine shot down into the water.

One of the German planes was shot down near the Hippodrome, where she

saw a sight I pray I may never see again. The wreck of the machine was partly burned, and still smouldering, and two tarpaulin covered objects, the pilot and his companion (the latter, I was afterwards told, a mere boy of seventeen or eighteen), were burned beyond recognition.[19]

The extensive work she did for charities, hospitals and troops, not to mention the recruiting enthusiasm at her concerts, were not referred to in her book. Nor did she record that her husband was knighted, and she became Lady de Frece, primarily as a result of his charitable work during the war, a prelude to his becoming a Conservative MP. Vesta performed concerts to raise money for war charities and especially for wounded soldiers, she encouraged men to enlist and she maintained correspondence with them at the front. Her scrapbooks of letters, playbills and newspaper cuttings include a wealth of correspondence to her, demonstrating her huge importance to the war effort. In one message to the Middlesex Regiment, she said that 'Since the beginning of the war I have been singing my song "The Army of to-day's all right" before audiences averaging twenty-five thousand people weekly, in London and the principal provincial cities of the United Kingdom'.[20] There were statements made at the time that a platoon of the regiment was called 'The Vesta Tilley Platoon'.

Working to raise money for the wounded was a key element of her very active contribution, giving small concerts and renditions as well as corresponding with the wounded directly. Private Castell wrote from his hospital bed in Newcastle, 'I only wish that I could come and hear you sing but that is impossible as I am too poorly. I hope and trust that you will find a few moments to spare to answer this little note.'[21] She did write back and he thanked her 'with all my heart and soul for your lovely gift and also for your photo which I shall cherish the longest day I live. I shall certainly take it with me when I go to the Front again'.[22] Vesta described what it was like receiving so many messages and letters:

You should see the letters I get from the boys at the Front. They send me such requests as 'Please Miss Tilley, will you wear this badge when you sing the Army of Today's Allright.'

If I were to wear all they send me I should be covered all over with badges. I'll tell you something about me I do wear. It was sent me in a battered bullet-ridden cigarette case, with a message that the sender found my Army song of great help in cheering him on to fight.[23]

Vesta started performing new songs, made a film and toured a short skit called *Six Days' Leave* about a soldier on leave. As well as performing she was very clearly also sending cigarettes and comforts, signed photographs and also recordings and gramophone players to the front in addition to the fifty hospitals for wounded soldiers who received a gramophone from her. However, sending a gramophone on to the BEF was not necessarily an easy operation. Captain Hynes, HQ XI Corps in France, thanked her in August 1917:

Very many thanks for the Gramophone which arrived safely yesterday. I am sorry that the one originally despatched did not turn up. The instrument will give very great pleasure to us here, it is an excellent one.[24]

Very likely some other unit snaffled it before it got to HQ! These were not just luxuries for the staff officers, however; Vesta was determined to get to the ordinary Tommy at the front, but again this did not always happen without a hitch.

Dear Miss Tilley, Would you be so kind as to forward enclosed letter to the gramophone people who manufactured the Gramophone you so kindly sent us some months ago. We don't know their address and have had a bit of a misfortune which has stopped the band playing. Furthermore, we ain't got a penny stamp between us so am sending in lieu a p.c. of the Boys who enjoy the music.
  Please oblige, Sgt Bird, 465 Field Company RE 46 Division.[25]

A couple of months later, in August 1917, Sergeant Bird wrote again:

Am pleased to acknowledge spare parts and records for Gramophone you so kindly sent us. This was some time ago of course but hope you will accept apologies for not giving receipt sooner. I assure you the 'phone is doing real good work and it may be a pleasure to let you know that not only my section but the whole company enjoy its music thus keeping us going. The Boys are more than pleased that they've records of your songs and wish me send you many thanks.[26]

Vesta Tilley had been born in the Blockhouse area of Worcester, a slum area where some of the poorest families eked out a living and lived on the edge of institutionalisation at the workhouse at the top of the Tallow Hill. Some fifty years later, it was the parish of Geoffrey Anketell Studdert Kennedy, or Woodbine Willie as he was famously known for handing out cigarettes to the soldiers at the front. He wrote prolifically, both poetry and prose, including one poem which reflected upon his role.

WOODBINE WILLIE
They gave me this name like their nature,
Compacted of laughter and tears,
A sweet that was born of the bitter,
A joke that was torn from the years.

Of their travail and torture, Christ's fools,
Atoning my sins with their blood,
Who grinned in their agony sharing
The glorious madness of God.

Their name I Let me hear it – the symbol
Of unpaid – unpayable debt,
For the men to whom I owed God's Peace,
I put off with a cigarette.

At various stages he was chaplain to the 157th Brigade in the 46th Division, and was in the 17th Brigade of the 24th Division in 1917 when he was awarded the Military Cross for action on the Messines Ridge, where he repeatedly retrieved wounded men from the shell holes in front of the trenches. During the final advance in 1918 he was with the 42nd Division. He also spent considerable time at the Army infantry schools, with training officers and NCOs.[27]

Studdert Kennedy arrived in Worcester to work in St Paul's parish in June 1914; it took him until December 1915 to get an appointment as a temporary chaplain in France. He wrote despatches from France, back to his parishioners whom he saw as having done him a favour in allowing him to go to the front. His first few were published in the *Berrows Worcestershire Journal*. In his first in early January 1916 he wrote, 'I thank God for sending me and you for letting me go.' He also detailed the extent to which he had tried to make Christmas as spiritually important in the trenches as it would have been at home, starting with a mass at 6.30 a.m.

At 9 a.m. I started out in a car to take services out in the country nearer the lines. It was pouring rain and the roads were very heavy. Everywhere along the road we met the troops, mud up to their knees, dripping wet, but always smiling, always with a greeting ready or a joke. After a service here, the padre then dashed into my car and off to another point five miles away. There it was the same more patient waiting men, more rain, more mud, more glory, more perfect Christmas peace.[28]

In his second despatch he went into some considerable detail about those last few hours before entraining to the front and was able to relate that he had recently 'struck a good many Worcester fellows'.

One lad named Baddely was at the first informal recruiting meeting which Frank Stanway and I held just after the war broke out and enlisted just afterward. I also came across some wireless men from just behind the Vicarage. I wrote home for them.[29]

At this stage of the war, Studdert Kennedy was based in Rouen, as town chaplain. On days when men were preparing to go forward to relieve the front line he would make his way to the station, where there was a large café providing a waiting area and refreshments for up to 1,200 men, who were often cooped up there all day until the evening.

It is generally growing dark by now and in the gloom a long train is standing – horse trucks – trucks piled with wood – and endless coaches. The men line up and all the place is alive with hoarse cries – one – two – three – four – down an endless line of men piled up with kit, with rifles slung on their shoulders. No more singing, no more human thought of love and home – this is business – the men are machines, splendid machines.

I slip out and arm myself with two great knapsacks – one is full of cigarettes, the other full of New Testaments … I begin at the top of the train and work down it going in each carriage. I look round the carriage and into their faces and I can always tell the man who has taken the trip before. You can see it in his eyes, they look different from the eyes of the boy sat next to him who is on his first journey to the front.

At last I am left alone looking after the tail lights of the disappearing train with a lump in my throat and a prayer in my hearts and a curse on the sin that causes war which grows more bitter every day. There is nothing glorious about this departure except the glory of their patience and grim determination. It is all sordid and filthy outside. Packed like herrings in an evil smelling carriage cramped and weary they will fall asleep from sheer exhaustion as the train creeps on its journey to the front.[30]

The Peace Treaty of Versailles was something that he found so very disappointing that he was moved to write 'Dead and Buried', which beautifully deifies the Tommy, his direct experience on the Western Front, and pours heavy scorn on the politician's conclusions:

> I have borne my cross through Flanders,
>   Through the broken heart of France,
> I have borne it through the deserts of the East;
>   I have wandered, faint and longing,
>   Through the human hosts that, thronging,
> Swarmed to glut their grinning idols with a feast.
>
> I was crucified in Cambrai,
>   And again outside Bapaume;
> I was scourged for miles along the Albert Road,
>   I was driven, pierced and bleeding,
>   With a million maggots feeding
> On the body that I carried as my load.

I have craved a cup of water,
   Just a drop to quench my thirst,
As the routed armies ran to keep the pace;
   But no soldier made reply
   As the maddened hosts swept by,
And a sweating straggler kicked me in the face.

There's no ecstasy of torture
   That the devils e'er devised,
That my soul has not endured unto the last;
   As I bore my cross of sorrow,
   For the glory of tomorrow,
Through the wilderness of battles that is past.

Yet my heart was still unbroken,
   And my hope was still unquenched,
Till I bore my cross to Paris through the crowd.
   Soldiers pierced me on the Aisne,
   But 'twas by the river Seine
That the statesmen brake my legs and made my shroud.

There they wrapped my mangled body
   In fine linen of fair words,
With the perfume of a sweetly scented lie,
   And they laid it in the tomb
   Of the golden-mirrored room,
'mid the many-fountained Gardens of Versailles.

With a thousand scraps of paper
   They made fast the open door,
And the wise men of the council saw it sealed.
   With the seal of subtle lying,
   They made certain of my dying,
Lest the torment of the peoples should be healed.

Then they set a guard of soldiers
    Night and day beside the Tomb,
Where the body of the Prince of Peace is laid,
    And the captains of the nations
    Keep the sentries to their stations,
Lest the statesman's trust from Satan be betrayed.

For it isn't steel and iron
    That men use to kill their God,
But the poison of a smooth and slimy tongue.
    Steel and iron tear the body,
    But it's oily sham and shoddy
That have trampled down God's spirit in the dung.[31]

Not long afterwards, he translated this experience of war into his work with the Industrial Mission, demonstrating just how far he had travelled since first he gave out Christmas mass near Rouen in 1915:

If we have learned anything from the past five years of hell, it surely ought to be that war never gets anything or anywhere. It is in every case a disaster which it is the bounden duty of every sane thinking person to hold out against till the very last ditch. It is and it never can be anything but a pure and unmitigated disaster.[32]

10

The Armistice and Post-War Memorialisation

News of the Armistice was greeted with great excitement, according to local press reports.[1] Worcester rejoiced, speeches were made at the Guildhall and a service was held at the cathedral. Work stopped at Ebenezer Bayliss and at Heenan and Froude where hooters sounded. There were church bells at Abberley, school bells and the national anthem at Alfrick; in Evesham flags and hooters were put out as people thronged the streets, and an exceptionally large congregation attended Colwall parish church for a service. At the infirmary, wounded Tommies joined in and at Battenhall Hospital they banged their mess tins in excitement. Chief constables throughout Worcestershire were informed by the Home Office that:

Masking of public lights may be removed forthwith.
Shading of house and shop lights withdrawn,
Fireworks and bonfires permitted subject to approval by military and police.
Public clocks may strike and bells ring at night.
The closing of restaurants at 9:30 and of theatres at 10:30 suspended.[2]

Malvern embraced the new freedoms.

To commemorate the signing of the armistice, Malvern made Thursday a holiday. In the morning several young ladies and wounded soldiers paraded the principal streets. Fancy costumes were worn and some of the party were on horseback. March music was played on drums and combs. National types were represented and Clowns and Pierrots were among the girls whose 'glad eye' battery brought about the surrender of Charlie Chaplin and many others too numerous to mention.

At 5:30 p.m. a torchlight procession was formed in Barnards Green and a move was made up the hill to Belle Vue Terrace where hundreds more fell in, Scouts with bands, the band of the Church Lad's Brigade, Girl Guides, wounded soldiers and young women in fancy costumes, on horse and foot, Britannia in a chariot, and Kaiser in a wicker chair, proceeded along Worcester Road to Link Top, and returned by way of Graham Road to Banards Green. On the common close to Poolbrook, the effigy of the Kaiser was placed on a bonfire, wearers of fancy costumes dancing around the flaming pile. Fireworks were discharged and the National Anthem, 'Rule Britannia' and 'Auld Lang Syne' were sung.[3]

But with the end of the war there was no end to the suffering. In a letter to the *Berrows Worcester Journal*, the officer commanding at Norton Barracks, Colonel Chichester, wrote,

I am ordered to expand the Hospital here to accommodate 600 wounded men. These men will be semi-convalescent men, it means I have to turn the barracks into Hospital wards. There are only the bare necessities at present available. I have an urgent want of games and playing cards, cigarettes, newspapers, periodicals. Also flowers to brighten up the wards would be most welcome.[4]

As with most large counties, commemorating the war in Worcestershire could be as divisive as it was widespread. In particular, competition between the county council plans and those of the city and other towns and villages threatened to limit the amount of money raised and spent on a range of memorials, including halls, crosses and charitable work. As early as 1916, the Mayor of Worcester proposed a scheme to build homes for disabled sailors and soldiers as a memorial, and this was adopted as a project by the city council, really as a fait accompli, at the end of

Victory parades and gatherings in Worcester. From *Berrows Worcestershire Journal*, 1918.

the war. Largely funded through public philanthropy, fetes, whist drives, a sports carnival, and donations, there was still concern that the homes – built on land belonging to Barbourne College and later renamed as 'Gheluvelt' Park – provided something the government should be doing. They were, perforce, only helping a few families, and ex-servicemen in particular argued that a more fitting memorial would be something that would benefit more people, such as halls, libraries or a swimming baths.[5] Discharged soldier Mr T. Grimmer, for instance, was concerned that 'the poor wounded soldiers were being "colonised", and discharged men were dead against it'.[6]

The county council started considering a county war memorial in 1917, but only once the war was over was a committee established to create a lasting memorial to those who had lost their lives.

From December 1918 onwards a series of meetings considered various sites for the county memorial, including a plan for a triumphal arch with a winged Victory at Worcester Cross. Others – all in Worcester – included Fort Royal Park, or the front of the Shirehall, moving the statue of Queen Victoria over to one side. The committee settled on space outside the cathedral since people had got used to there being a temporary cenotaph there since 1918. Even that was a source of discussion, the proposed architect being concerned that the size of the proposal would be dwarfed by both the cathedral and the South African memorial alongside.

Disabled Worcestershire basket makers in 1919. From *Berrows Worcestershire Journal*.

Posters for the county War Memorial meeting in 1918. (With thanks to Worcestershire Archive and Archaeology Service)

A key aspect to the county memorial was the relief fund for disabled ex-servicemen and their families. While of some practical help, it was not universally thought of as a 'memorial'. T. W. Parkes wrote to the local paper, complaining that

Worcester Cenotaph in 1919. From *Berrows Worcestershire Journal*.

a memorial was something to preserve memory, and with all due respect to the Committee and to the widows and dependents of the fallen, [he] was absolutely and positively against the doles which had been given out of the fund.[7]

Despite that perspective, it soon became clear that the administration of the fund was quite restricted. In response to claims put forward to the committee, Mr Bird, the secretary, explained his reasons for refusal:

The difficulty I am now in is to select the cases which should be sent to the Incumbents as typical, the 3 cases which Mrs Wodehouse gave me as coming from you do not appear to me or to Mr. Bund [Chairman] to be at all suitable.

1. Mrs Hamilton. She is living in the City of Worcester and is the widow of a RE she therefore does not at first sight become eligible for her husband did not belong to a Worcestershire Unit and prima facie was not a Worcestershire resident.

2. Sergeant Wilson. He has received £75 from the King's Fund and £75 from the OCA and is apparently provided for.

3. Demobilised Soldier (Bowen) This man had received £50 from the OCA and is apparently provided for.

According to the Lord Lieutenant's Circular the cases to be helped are those which are ineligible for any other Fund and Mr. Bund has directed me not to do anything further.[8]

There were two other elements to the county's memorial – the writing of a history of the eighteen battalions of the Worcestershire Regiment, and a stained-glass window inside the cathedral, with a book listing those killed from Worcestershire. This was later expanded to include five brass memorial plates to those killed in the Royal Navy, the Worcestershire Regiment, the Artillery, the Yeomanry and one for other units. The committee's main concern was to obtain funds for all these projects and the Lord Lieutenant, Lord Coventry, issued an appeal for subscriptions in 1918 to raise £1,000. A subscription list for those giving more than £10 was published but a number of responses in early 1919 demonstrate the problems that the county committee had in convincing people to contribute. At one extreme was the telegram from the veterans of 2nd Worcestershires, the unit that had fought at Gheluvelt, addressed to the Worcester mayor, Alderman Carlton, who had lost a son in the war:

Twelve Hundred county discharged disabled and crippled sailors and soldiers emphatically protest against County war memorial meeting to raise funds for church tablets and records and for so called charitable purposes by aristocrats of the city and county.[9]

On the other hand, some, like Miss Elliott, wrote in to ask how to contribute:

Dear Sir, Will you kindly send me one of the printed notices of the Scheme for the Worcestershire County War memorial as I should like to send something towards it. And I should be glad of one or two spare copies to give away.[10]

Viscountess Lifford expressed the concern that £10 was too high a sum to pay:

I cannot subscribe to the Fund being only able to promise £2-2-0. There is our own War Memorial in the village to be subscribed to besides many claims on one's depleted income.[11]

A common theme among concerned inhabitants of the county was that their local area or parish was trying to raise money for a local memorial as well, and there was, in fact, a competition growing up with the county's proposals. Alice Baird was keen to contribute but wanted to know first what scheme was proposed for the West Malvern War Memorial.[12] The 'competition' from villages and towns across the county in erecting war memorials was widespread and many chose memorial halls because, in the words of the Vicar of Ombersley, Revd Crawford, 'A cross would be forgotten in ten years, but a public room which might be a centre of education and recreation would be of benefit to posterity and be evidence of gratitude to the men.'[13] Honourable Secretary Mr Bird, in writing to Miss Neale of Bromsgrove, emphasised that the executive committee regard the multiplication of local War memorials as unfortunate because if the proposed fund is to be of any real value to the disabled Officers and Men and the Dependents of those who have fallen it is essential that it should be of considerable size, and that any local effort should be in addition to and not in substitution for the County War Memorial. I must also point out that the County War Memorial will of necessity be a Memorial for each and every district in the County, and each and every district will have an equal right to participate.[14]

The subscription list, which included commitments of £200 from the Earl of Coventry, £100 from the Deerhursts and Viscount Cobham, £100 from the Eyres Monsells, MP and veteran, was headed by £250 from Captain Guy Edwards of the Worcestershire Regiment. The Sergeants' Mess in the 6th Battalion gave £15, while the Yeomanry sergeants afforded £12. Rather disappointingly, Willis Bund, chairman of the county council, would only contribute a £10 subscription, which just got him onto the published list.[15] The list itself was controversial, however, and the Vicar of Tredington, W. A. Edwards, was typical of many who responded to the appeal:

I am in full sympathy with it but it is impossible for me to make a large contribution as I am giving a substantial donation to the Memorial in my own parish and also other like objects. I see that no contributions under £10 are entered on your list. If you can accept the guinea, I shall be pleased to send you one, but if your net is only for big fish I am not in that category'.[16]

The stained-glass window was unveiled on Armistice Day, 1921, the war memorial outside the cathedral a year later. An ex-serviceman representative from each parish was invited, though expenses were not paid. The History, by Stacke, was published in 1929 and some 2,890 copies were sent out. The History Committee Fund's costs over-ran, however, and had to be made up from the War Memorial Committee main fund. Nonetheless, copies were still being sold to ex-members of the regiment at the discounted rate of 12/- as late as 1935.

In 1920 a charitable movement spread to Worcestershire encouraging towns to adopt a devastated town in France or Flanders, as a means of supporting them after the war. The British League of Help recommended these adopting towns to look to places where need was highest and that had links with the men killed, now lying in cemeteries or commemorated on the Western Front. The British League of Help persuaded four towns in Worcestershire to pursue an adoption – Malvern of Landrecies, Evesham of Hébuterne, Worcester of Gouzeaucourt, and Stourbridge adopted Grandcourt. To a greater or lesser degree these town adoptions proceeded through the 1920s. Worcester summoned up just about enough money to fund a wind-driven water pump manufactured by 'Pumpy' Thomas, the type commonly seen around the county. The arrangements between Worcester and Gouzeaucourt would have benefited from better translation facilities. In correspondence to his counterpart in France, Worcester's mayor confirmed he was forwarding £1,100 – which was read in Gouzeaucourt as *onze cent livres*, and they could not understand why the 'generous but quite mad English' were sending 1,100 books to help the ruined village recover![17]

Evesham and Hébuterne enjoyed an on-off relationship. The mayor and a delegation from Evesham visited Hébuterne at the end of September 1920 and had a tour of the area, which was described as a 'scene of desolation'. Noting the village's agricultural and other needs, he established a committee and started fundraising. In December 1920, he was able to inform the League of Help:

We held a Committee meeting on Tuesday afternoon when arrangements were made for collecting goods with a view to sending off to Hebtuerne as soon as possible and I will let you know as soon as we are ready to forward things from here. I am today writing to the Maire of Hébuterne with a further draft of 2,000 francs and I am also asking about the livestock. We have four cows, two goats, and one sow which can be sent as soon as we can get permission, first from the French Minister of Agriculture and secondly a Certificate from the English Minister of Agriculture. In the meantime I am asking the Maire of Hébuterne at the suggestion of the Committee, whether it would not be better to postpone sending the livestock until the Spring, or the middle of March, as they will probably have considerable difficulty out there providing fodder and shelter during the cold weather. In the meantime the owners have set these cattle aside and are having them taken care of for the purposes of exporting. They will all be in-calf heifers.[18]

Having expressed their interest, another war charity – the Fund for War Devastated Villages – also contacted Evesham Borough seeking funds towards their own scheme of assisting French towns, but Councillor New stayed loyal to the British League of Help. He was congratulated for making the effort to visit the area himself:

I can well imagine your feelings when you saw for yourself the conditions at Hébuterne, and realised what there is to do in the Devastated Area. Only those who have seen can really understand.[19]

However, by June 1922, relations had deteriorated. The secretary of the League commiserated with Evesham's mayor:

I am surprised that the Mairie of Hebuterne did not write to you on the arrival of the cattle. We have complaints from time to time of the negligence of French Mayors in these matters, and we make a point of forwarding these complaints to the Ministre des Regions Libertees who brings offenders to book.[20]

A more positive relationship was enjoyed by some boys of the sixth form at King Edward's School, Stourbridge, who joined a large party of schoolboys who made the trip to France at Whitsuntide, 1923, stayed in Paris and then went on to their own places of adoption. The boys – M. W. R. Darke, F. Bourne, H. Unitt, J. Jones, S. R. Wooldridge, G. W. Eason, N. Finney and A. Tipper – reported back to their school magazine, and the local paper:

On Monday morning after another early breakfast, we boarded motors and set off for Amiens. By the time we had reached Soissons, where we were to lunch, more than half the chars-a-bancs which had left Paris had broken down, and the occupants of these had been forced to pack themselves in the remaining three. Near Montdidier we spent a few minutes on the battlefields and succeed in finding several German helmets, a pile of unused cartridges and hand grenades, and a dug-out which was entirely intact. We arrived at our destination about midnight without lights and thoroughly tired out.[21]

Since the main aim of the trip was to visit the different places adopted by the full range of the group of 300 schoolboys, the party divided the following day.

Next morning, Tuesday, we boarded a train which was to convey several parties to their respective 'adopted' towns and villages. The Stourbridge party was, however, compelled to leave the train at Beaucourt-Hamel and take to horse-drawn vehicles. These proceeded slowly along an exceedingly 'bumpy' road which was bordered on either side by dead and splintered stumps of trees. On our arrival at the entrance of the village a gun was fired twice, which stimulated the movements of the quadrupeds drawing the gigs. We passed underneath an archway decorated with green branches and bearing an inscription which, being translated, read, 'Welcome to the children of Stourbridge, our helper and protector.' Followed by the greater part of the inhabitants of the village we proceeded to the Mayor's Office. Here we distributed parcels of linen, bought with Stourbridge money, to the heads of each family. They were received with profuse thanks and a small child presented us with a bouquet of flowers. This presentation was received with a cheer, and Mr Aggleton, true always to the 'entente cordiale', took the child in his arms and kissed him on both cheeks.

After dinner in the Mayor's Office, we inspected the school, the number of pupils attending it being about fourteen. All these children had been given a half holiday in our honour. The Mayor and Mayoress and the children conducted us over the battlefields to the British Stump Road Cemetery. We picked up several helmets and bayonets as souvenirs. We were then allowed to explore the battlefields, but owing to a shower of rain we returned to tea.[22]

Worcestershire's breadth of memorialisation was not untypical of a rural county. The legacy, still seen today in monuments and buildings and reawakened in links with specific towns, demonstrates that despite the obvious difficulties of managing and administering a fitting memorial, the county's efforts were a reasonable response that attempted to meet most needs and aspirations of the range of communities and population.

A range of emotions, developments and activities marked the years following the First World War; everyday life was coloured by and measured against wartime experiences. Worcestershire's landscape, in social, cultural and economic terms, was altered and the conflict left its legacy on individuals, families and communities as they tried to make sense of their memories and their losses. The poetry of Worcestershire poet Geoffrey Studdert Kennedy spoke to the very mixed emotions of the inter-war years.

WASTE

Waste of Muscle, waste of Brain,
Waste of Patience, waste of Pain,
Waste of Manhood, waste of Health,
Waste of Beauty, waste of Wealth,
Waste of Blood, and waste of Tears,
Waste of Youth's most precious years,

Waste of ways the Saints have trod,
Waste of Glory, waste of God, –
War.

WAR

There's a soul in the Eternal,
Standing stiff before the King.
There's a little English maiden Sorrowing
There's a proud and tearless woman,
Seeing pictures in the fire.
There's a broken battered body
On the wire.

Notes

1 Worcestershire and the Outbreak of War

1. A. G. Bradley and T. Tyndale (1909), *Worcestershire*, London: A&C Black, pp 1–24; *Official County Handbook* (1957), Cheltenham: J. Burrow& Co, p. 35.
2. T. C. Turbeville (1852), *Worcestershire in the Nineteenth Century*, London: Green and Longmans, pp 1–29.
3. Tynedale and Bradley, *ibid*. pp 1–24.
4. Turbeville, pp 312–7.
5. R. C. Gaut (1939), *A History of Worcestershire Agriculture and Rural Evolution*, Worcester: Littlebury Press, p. 382.
6. *Ibid*. p. 399.
7. *Ibid*. pp. 401–2.
8. *Burrow's Worcestershire County Guide*, 1899, p. 12.
9. *Worcester Daily Times*, 9, 10 and 21 August 1914.
10. *Worcester Daily Times*, 21 August 1914.
11. *Worcester Daily Times*, 11 August 1914.
12. *Kidderminster Shuttle*, 1 and 15 August 1914.
13. *Kidderminster Shuttle*, 8 August 1914.
14. Tynedale and Bradley, p. 24.
15. *Worcester Daily Times*, 10 August 1914.
16. *Worcester Daily Times*, 3 August 1914.
17. The main reference work for the Worcestershire Regiment in the war is the History written as part of the county war memorial, published in Captain H. Stacke (1928), *The Worcestershire Regiment in the Great War*, Kidderminster: Cheshire & Sons.

18. *Berrows Journal*, 19 September 1914, p.7.
19. *Berrows Journal*, 26 September 1914, p.5.
20. Stacke, pp. 1–23.
21. Stacke, pp. 42–51.
22. Pte G. F. Gilbert, 8th Worcestershire Battalion, *Berrows Worcestershire Journal*, 3 October 1914, p.3.
23. 'C' (1926), *The Yeomanry Cavalry of Worcestershire 1914–1922*, Stourbridge: Mark and Moody Ltd, p.5.
24. *Ibid.*
25. The extracts published here come by kind permission of Dr John Godrich; they are from Victor Godrich, *Mountains of Moab: The Diary of a Cavalryman with the Queen's own Worcestershire Hussars*, edited and published by Dr John Godrich in 2011.
26. *Worcester Daily Times*, 4 September 1914.
27. M. Anderson (1936), *A Few More Memories*, London: Hutchinson pp. 145–6.
28. *Birmingham Daily Post*, 21 July 1915.
29. WAAS WCC minutes, 14 December 1914.
30. *Birmingham Daily Post*, 21 July 1915.
31. *The Birmingham Evening Mail*, 14 May 1915.
32. *Evening Dispatch*, 31 October 1917.

2 The Yeomanry in the Middle East

1. A. Bruce (2002), *The Last Crusade: The Palestine Campaign in the First World War*, London: John Murray pp. 3–6.
2. *Ibid.*, p. 8.
3. *Ibid.*, p. 11.
4. *Ibid.*, p. 1.
5. *Ibid.*, p. 13.
6. 'C' (1926), *The Yeomanry Cavalry of Worcestershire 1914–1922* Stourbridge: Mark and Moody Ltd, p.18.
7. *Ibid.*, pp.30–38.
8. *Ibid.*, p. 46.
9. The extracts published here come by kind permission of Dr John Godrich; they are from Victor Godrich, *Mountains of Moab: The Diary of a Cavalryman with the Queen's own Worcestershire Hussars*, edited and published by Dr John Godrich in 2011.
10. Mercian Regiment Museum Ref. 2006–363.

11. *Last Crusade* pp. 36–7.
12. Letter from Cyril Sladden, 15 February 1917. WAAS ref. 705:1037 BA 9520.
13. *Last Crusade*, p. 2.
14. *Worcester Daily Times*, 2 March 1917.
15. Jack Preece, letter to his parents, 30 December 1915. WAAS ref. 705:138 BA 5334.

3 Agriculture and Food Production

1. *Worcester Daily Times*, 9 August 1914.
2. *Worcester Daily Times*, 21 August 1914.
3. *Worcester Daily Times*, 11 September 1914.
4. *Worcester Daily Times*, 21 August 1914.
5. R. C. Gaut (1939), *A History of Worcestershire Agriculture and Evolution of Rural Society in Worcestershire*, Littlebury Press.
6. Letter in the Pershore branch of the Worcestershire War Agricultural Executive Committee, WAAS ref. 2592:2 BA 179.
7. *Worcester Herald*, 25 December 1915.
8. *Worcester Herald*, 12 December 1914.
9. *Worcester Daily News*, 3 November 1916.
10. *Worcester Daily News*, 27 November 1914.
11. *Country Life Magazine*, 16 March 1915.
12. *Worcester Herald*, 12 June 1915.
13. *Birmingham Daily Post*, Monday 21 June 1915.
14. *Worcester Daily Times*, 8 December 1915.
15. 'Field Work in Elmley Castle' in *The Mermaid*, 1915–16, pp. 23–4, by kind permission of the Cadbury Research Library, Birmingham University.
16. *Worcester Daily Times*, 8 December 1915.
17. 'Strawberry pickers at Elmley Castle' in *The Mermaid*, 1916–17, pp. 12–13.
18. *Worcester Daily Times*, 5 October 1916.
19. *Berrows Worcester Journal*, 25 May 1917.
20. *Berrows Worcester Journal*, 10 March 1917.
21. *Hansard*, 1 July 1918 [http://hansard.millbanksystems.com/search].
22. *Evesham Journal*, 1918.

4 Women in Wartime

1. *Worcester Herald*, 8 August 1914.
2. *Ibid.*
3. *Worcester Daily Times*, 10 August 1914.
4. *Worcester Daily Times*, 14 August 1914.
5. *Worcester Herald*, 27 November 1915.
6. *Worcester Daily Times*, 11 December 1914.
7. *Worcester Daily Times*, 30 October 1914.
8. *Worcester Daily Times*, 8 December 1915.
9. *Worcester Herald*, 14 November 1914.
10. *Worcester Daily Times*, 26 November 1914.
11. *Worcester Daily Times*, 27 November 1914.
12. *Ibid.*
13. *Worcester Daily Times*, 11 August 1914.
14. *Worcester Daily Times*, 2 October 1914.
15. *Worcester Daily Times*, 21 August 1914.
16. *Worcester Daily Times*, 9 October 1914.
17. *Worcester Herald*, 16 January 1915.
18. *Worcester Herald*, 16 January 1915.
19. *Worcester Daily Times*, 9 October 1915.
20. *Worcester Daily Times*, 10 August 1914.
21. *Worcester Daily Times*, 11 September 1914.
22. *Worcester Daily News*, 25 September 1914.
23. *Worcester Herald*, 12 June 1915.
24. *Worcester Herald*, 17 July 1915.
25. *Worcester Daily Times*, 3 November 1916.
26. *Ibid.*
27. Hagley Hall Scrapbook report of Worcester, Jan. 1918, Worcestershire Archive and Archaeology Service, ref. 899:1500 BA 14526.
28. *Worcester Daily Times*, 4 May 1917.
29. Kidderminster War Savings Committee Scrapbook, WAAS ref. 899:310 BA10470/537.
30. *Worcester Daily News*, 1 June 1917.
31. Newspaper extract in Malvern War Saving Committee Scrapbook, 1 June 1917, WAAS ref. 004.9 BA 8039.
32. *Ibid.*
33. Hagley Hall Scrapbook, autumn 1917, WAAS ref. 899:1500 BA 14526.

34. Lavinia Talbot diaries, 26 July 1915, held in WAAS ref 705:104 BA
    15492.

5 Dear Mother, Dear Wife

1. Extracts from Dispatches Worcestershire Archive and Archaeology
   Service, ref. 705;948 BA 8763.
2. Worcestershire Regimental Museum, ref. 2007–136. Jack Bird
   Pte 34682. 6th Battalion then 2nd Battalion Worcs, transferred
   to Labour Corps. Finished in D company, 13th Platoon of 14th
   Worcestershire Pioneers, 415243.
3. Extracts here from WAAS, ref 705.1076 BA 9733. Transcripts of
   letters written by a private soldier to his wife.
4. Letters and images in the private collection of Sean Brown by
   whose kind permission they are reproduced here.

6 Voices of Some Very Different Experiences of War

1. Letter on life in the Navy in 1918, Worcestershire Archive and
   Archaeology Service (WAAS), ref. 970.5:1252 BA 1252.
2. September 1916, WAAS ref. 899.116 BA 5225 also reproduced.
   [http://www.worcestershireregiment.com/wr.php?main=inc/
   whs_chance_5.]
3. *Ibid.*
4. Copies of the diaries, letters and photographs of A. C. Pepper have
   been kindly supplied by his granddaughter Lorna Cameron.
5. For further details on James Whale see [http://www.birminghammail.
   co.uk/whats-on/things-to-do/james-whale-exhibition-charts-the-
   life-384719].
6. National Archives, ref. wo/161/98/216.
7. John Willis-Bund was Chairman of the County Council from 1893.
   He also ran a legal practice in London and was Chairman of the
   Quarter Sessions of both Worcestershire and Cardiganshire. He
   was a County Alderman and Chairman of the influential Education
   Committee from its inception in 1903 for the next twenty years. It
   was in his role as Chairman of the County Council for thirty-five
   years that he exerted most influence including a significant role

in the County's governance of the war effort and agriculture in particular between 1914 and 1918.

8. WAAS, ref. b705:730 BA 6009.
9. WAAS, ref. 200.01 BA22/24, p.211.
10. WAAS, ref. b705:730 BA 6009.
11. WAAS, ref. b705:730 BA 6009.
12. WAAS, ref. b705:730 BA 6009.
13. WAAS, ref. b705:730 BA 6009.
14. WAAS, ref. b75:1120/3/ix, BA:10142.
15. WAAS, BA10142/2/iv/10.
16. WAAS, BA10142/2/iv/11–20.

7 The Home Front

1. *Kidderminster Shuttle*, 1 August 1914.
2. *Kidderminster Shuttle*, 8 August 1914.
3. Worcestershire Archive and Archaeology Service (WAAS), ref. 9:51 BA259, 11 Sept. 1914.
4. WAAS, ref. 200.01 BA22/22, p.900–904.
5. *Worcester Daily Times*, 11 September 1914.
6. *Worcester Daily Times*, 17 September 1914.
7. WAAS, Lavinia Talbot diaries, vol. xxxiii 1914, ref 705:104 BA 15492.
8. *Worcester Daily Times*, 2 October 1914.
9. WAAS, ref. 200.01 BA 22/22, pp. 906, 923 and 924.
10. WAAS, ref. 200.01 BA 22/22 p. 620.
11. WAAS, ref. 200.01 BA22/23, p. 27.
12. WAAS, ref. b705:730 BA: 6009.
13. WAAS, ref. 200.01 BA22/23, p. 383.
14. WAAS, ref. b705:1120/3/ix BA:10142.
15. *Worcestershire Echo*, 29 August 1916.
16. WAAS, ref. b705:730 BA 6009.
17. WAAS, ref. 494.5 BA10917/33.
18. WAAS, ref. 494.5 BA10917/33.
19. *Worcester Herald*, 22 March 1916.
20. WAAS, ref. 200.01 BA22/24, pp. 4–6.
21. *Worcester Daily Times*, 3 March 1916.
22. *Worcester Daily Times*, 3 November 1916.
23. *Kidderminster Shuttle*, 30 March 1918.

24. WAAS, ref:494.5 BA10917/33.
25. Kidderminster War Savings Committee Scrapbook, WAAS ref. 899:310 BA10470/537.
26. *Ibid.*

8 Worcestershire's Role in Wartime Medical Care

1. Letters of Arthur Sladden, a civil surgeon in the Royal Army Medical Corps in France, WAAS ref. 705:1037 BA 9520/3.
2. L. Binyon (1918) *Doubtless in France*. [http://www.archive.org/stream/fordauntlessfranoobiny/fordauntlessfranoobiny_djvu.txt]
3. WAAS ref. 705.1076 BA 9733. Transcripts of letters written by a private soldier to his wife.
4. *Worcester Daily Times*, 2 October 1914.
5. V. Godrich (2011), *Hills of Moab: The Diary of a Cavalry Man with the Queen's Own Worcestershire Hussars 1908–1919*, edited and published by Dr J. Godrich, reproduced by kind permission of Dr J. Godrich.
6. *Birmingham Mail*, 23 October 1915.
7. Letter from Stourbridge VAD hospital. [http://www.1914-1918.net/southerngen.htm]
8. Hartlebury VAD Hospital Autograph Book, in the Hurd Library at Hartlebury Castle.
9. *Ibid.*
10. *Ibid*
11. *Worcester Herald*, 8 August 1914.
12. Battenhall Hospital Autograph Book, held in the Infirmary Museum Worcester.
13. *Ibid.*
14. Hartlebury VAD Hospital Autograph Book, in the Hurd Library at Hartlebury Castle.
15. Evesham Manor Hospital Rule Book from the private collection of the Rudge family.
16. V. Godrich (2011), *Hills of Moab: The Diary of a Cavalry Man with the Queen's Own Worcestershire Hussars 1908–1919*, edited and published by D. J. Godrich.
17. *Evesham Journal* extract in in Mrs Rudge's Scrapbook from the private collection of the Rudge family.
18. *Ibid.*

9 Famous Faces of Wartime Worcestershire

1. Captain H. Stacke (1928), *The Worcestershire Regiment in the Great War*, Kidderminster: Cheshire & Sons.
2. *Berrows Worcester Journal*, 1 December 1917.
3. Unweeded correspondence, Lyttelton Collection Worcestershire Archive and Archaeology Service, ref. 705:104 BA15492.
4. *Ibid.*
5. WAAS ref. b705:730 BA 6009.
6. *Ibid.*
7. *Ibid.*
8. *Ibid.*
9. Letters to Edward Elgar, no.6403 from Col. Cecil Coles, 15 August 1916, Elgar Birthplace Museum Trust.
10. Letters to Edward Elgar, no.6402 from John Godfrey Coles, 2 November 1916, Elgar Birthplace Museum Trust.
11. A. Bishop and M. Bostridge (eds) (1999), *Letters from a Lost Generation: First World War Letters of Vera Brittain and Four Friends*, Abacus Roland Leighton to Vera Brittain, 27 August 1915, p. 149.
12. *Ibid.* Leighton to Brittain, 6 September 1915, p. 160.
13. *Ibid.* Leighton to Brittain, 7 September 1915, p. 161.
14. *Ibid.* Leighton to Brittain, 18 September 1915, p.169.
15. *Ibid.* Leighton to Brittain, 30 November 1915, pp.192–3.
16. *Ibid.* Leighton to Brittain, 9 December 1915, pp.198-9.
17. *Ibid.* Leighton to Brittain, 13 December 1915, p. 199.
18. Lady de Frece (1934), *Recollections of Vesta Tilley*, London: Hutchinson.
19. *Ibid.*
20. Vesta Tilley, scrapbook of letters and cuttings, WAAS Ref. b899:1400 BA14233/1/1-71.
21. *Ibid.*
22. *Ibid.*
23. *Ibid.*
24. *Ibid.*
25. *Ibid.*
26. *Ibid.*
27. W. Purcell, *Woodbine Willie: A Biography*, London: Hodder and Stoughton 1962.
28. Studdert Kennedy despatches, collected cuttings of January and February 1916. WAAS Ref. 705:948 BA8763/2(ii).

29. *Ibid.*
30. *Ibid.*
31. *Dead and Buried* (1920), G. A. Studdert Kennedy in *Peace Rhymes of a Padre*, Hodder and Stoughton.
32. *The Best of Studdert Kennedy: Selected from His Own Writings by a* Friend (1947), Hodder & Stoughton.

10 The Armistice and Post-War Memorialisation

1. *Berrows Worcester Journal*, 16 November 1918.
2. *Worcester Daily Times*, 11 November 1918.
3. *Worcestershire Daily Times*, 15 November 1918.
4. *Berrows Worcester Journal*, 16 November 1918.
5. Jo Baldwin (1998), *'An objection to bricks and mortar?': The Processes of Memorialisation in Worcestershire 1916–1922*, unpub. thesis, University of Worcester.
6. *Berrows Worcester Journal*, 4 January 1919.
7. *Berrows Worcester Journal*, 20 August 1921.
8. Joint War Memorial Committee Correspondence, Worcestershire County Council, WAAS Ref. 259.9:26 BA3239/3 Letter no. 12.
9. *Ibid.* Letter no. 16.
10. *Ibid.* Letter no.18.
11. *Ibid.* Letter no. 17.
12. *Ibid.* Letter no. 13.
13. *Berrows Worcester Journal*, 15 February 1919.
14. Joint War Memorial Committee Correspondence, Worcestershire County Council, WAAS Ref. 259.9:26 BA3239/3 Letter no. 11.
15. Joint War Memorial Committee Correspondence, Worcestershire County Council, WAAS Ref. 259.9:26 BA3239/4.
16. Joint War Memorial Committee Correspondence, Worcestershire County Council, WAAS Ref. 259.9:26 BA3239/3 Letter no. 21.
17. *Berrows Worcester Journal*, 26 November 1921.
18. Evesham Borough Council correspondence BA1344, 10 December 1920.
19. *Ibid.* 18 October 1920.
20. *Ibid.* 9 June 1922.
21. Stourbridge Edwardian Vol 1, 1922–1924, pp. 121–8.
22. *Ibid.*

Bibliography

Andrews, M. (1997), *The Acceptable Face of Feminism: The Women's Institute Movement*, London: Lawrence and Wishart.

Andrews, M., C. Bagot-Jewitt and N. Hunt (2011), *Lest We Forget: Remembrance and Commemoration*, Stroud: History Press.

Andrews, M. and J. Lomas (2014), *Home Front: Myths Images and Forgotten Experiences*, Basingstoke: Palgrave Macmillan.

Beckett, I., *Home Front 1914–18: How Britain Survived the Great War*, London: National Archives.

Bourke J. (1996), *Dismembering Bodies: Men's Bodies Britain and the Great War*, London Reaktion Books.

Brittain, V. (1933, reprinted 2004), *Testament of Youth*, London: Virago Press.

Brittain, V. (1981), *Chronicle of Youth: Vera Brittain's Diary 1913–17*, London: Victor Gollancz Ltd.

Emden, R. van (2006), *Boy Soldiers of the Great War*, London: Headline.

Farrar-Hockley, A. (1967, reprinted 1998), *Death of an Army*, Ware: Wordsworth Editions.

Goodall, F. (2010), *We Will Not Go to War: Conscientious Objection for the World Wars*, Stroud: History Press.

Gregory, A. (2005), *The Last Great War: British Society and the First World War*, Cambridge: Cambridge University Press.

Grundy, M. (1997), *A Fiery Glow in the Darkness: Woodbine Willie Padre and Poet*, London: Osborne Books Ltd.

Hallett, C. E. (2009), *Containing Trauma: Nursing Work in the First World War*, Manchester: Manchester University Press.

Howkins, A. (1991), *Reshaping Rural England: A Social History 1850–1925*, London: Hutchinson.

Howkins, A. (2003), *The Death of Rural England*, London: Routledge.

Humphries, S. and R. van Emden (2003), *All Quiet on the Home Front: An Oral History of the First World War*, London: Hodder Headline.

MacDonald, L. (1989), *1914: The Days of Hope*, London: Penguin.

McDermott, J. (2011), *British Military Service Tribunals 1916–18*, Manchester: Manchester University Press.

McEwen, Y. (2006), *It's a Long Way to Tipperary: British and Irish Nurses in the Great War*, Dunfermline: Cualann Press.

Mansfield, N. (2001), *English Farmworkers and Local Patriotism 1900–1930*, Aldershot: Palgrave.

Pankhurst, S. (1932), *Home Front*, republished by London: Cressert Library.

Roper, M. (2009), *The Secret Battle: Emotional Survival in the Great War*, Manchester: Manchester University Press.

Strachan, H. (2001), *The First World War Vol. 1: To Arms*, Oxford: Oxford University Press.

Sudworth, G. (1984), *The Great Little Tilley: Vesta Tilley and Her Times*, Luton: Courtney Publications.

Winter, J. (1995), *Sites of Memory Sites of Mourning*, Cambridge: Cambridge University Press.

Winter, J. (1995, reprinted 2003), *The Great War and the British People*, Basingstoke: Palgrave.

Woodward, D. R. (2006) *Forgotten Soldiers of the First World War*, Stroud: History Press.

Acknowledgements

There are a number of people and organisations whose kind help has enabled this book to come into existence.

First and foremost, the staff and volunteers at Worcestershire Archive and Archaeology Service and other local archives and libraries, including: Paul Hudson, Julian Pugh, Rosemary Johnson and the Hurd Library, John Paddock and The Mercian Regiment Museum, Mark Macleod at the Infirmary, the Elgar Birthplace Museum and the Museums Worcestershire Service.

Worcester University students past and present did some admirable work trawling through local newspapers and transcribing letters, and particular thanks goes to Roz Crombie, Jo Baldwin, Sharon Randall and Jessie Gleeson for their help.

The authors would particularly like to thank a number of individuals for kindly allowing us access to their family's research papers, photographs and archives, extracts of which we have reproduced in this book. These include: the Rudge family, Lorna Cameron, Michael Hall, John Godrich and Sean Brown.

Finally our thanks are due to the friends, families and colleagues who have given us the space to complete this book; we hope you will all find something of interest in it.

About the Authors

Professor Maggie Andrews is a cultural historian at the University of Worcester, focusing on the Home Front in the First and Second World Wars. She leads the theme of *Gender and the Home Front* for the Voices of War and Peace: the Great War and its Legacy Engagement Centre and is an adviser to the BBC's World War One at Home project in the West Midlands.

Dr Adrian Gregson is an archivist and historian working for Worcestershire Archive and Archaeology Service at The Hive. Originally from Lancashire, his PhD looked at 1/7th Battalion King's Liverpool Regiment during the First World War. He is currently leading a Heritage Lottery funded project on Worcestershire's First World War commemorations.

Dr John Peters is Head of Academic Practice at Newman University, Birmingham. His PhD addressed government industrial and economic planning during the First World War and he has successfully supervised a number of PhDs on the First World War. He lives in beautiful west Worcestershire.

Index

Also available from Amberley Publishing

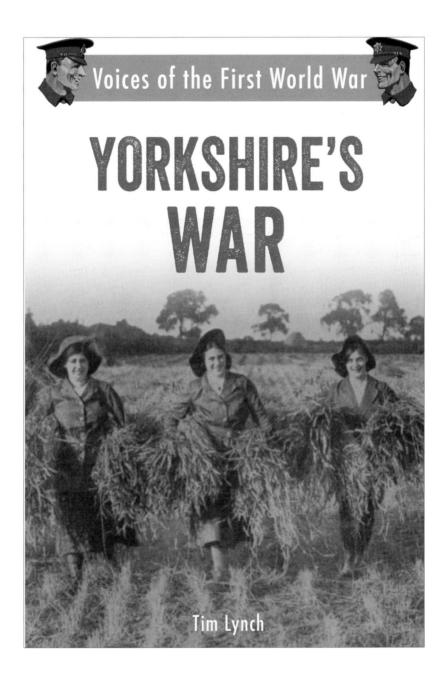

Voices of the First World War

YORKSHIRE'S WAR

Tim Lynch

Available from all good bookshops or to order direct
Please call **01453-847-800**
www.amberleybooks.com

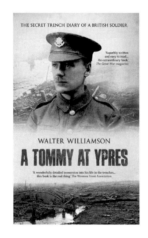
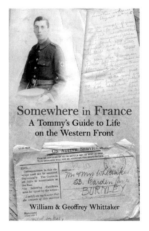